The Eloquence of Edward Everett:
America's Greatest Orator

Edward Everett,
Statesman and Orator

The Eloquence
of Edward Everett
America's Greatest
Orator

Richard A. Katula

Dorchester Historical Society, 2009

ISBN: 978-0-615-27556-7

Contents

Statue of Edward Everett
Dorchester, Massachusetts

Acknowledgments

The Eloquence of Edward Everett: America's Greatest Orator is made possible through the support of the National Endowment for the Humanities, Northeastern University, and the Dorchester Historical Society. When in 2007 the NEH so generously supported the author's proposal to conduct a workshop for community college faculty on the American Lyceum movement of the mid-nineteenth century and the oratory of this Golden Age, certain names came immediately to mind: Ralph Waldo Emerson, Henry David Thoreau, Lucy Stone, Frederick Douglass, John B. Gough, Angelina and Sarah Grimke, Wendell Phillips, and Edward Everett. There were many others, of course, but with these orators serving as illustrations, we believed, the story of the public forum movement could be told in an entertaining and informative manner. Reading the evaluations following the two workshops, it became clear that while Everett was one of the least known of this group, his story was the highlight of the program. The original urge to write this book arose out of the curiosity of those who participated in the NEH workshops to know more about Edward Everett, in particular about his legendary career as an orator.

Northeastern University, my academic home for the past nineteen years, has encouraged and underwritten this text. The Provost's Office provided a generous grant to fund the editing phase. James Stellar, former dean of the College of Arts and Sciences, long supported my work with the National Endowment for the Humanities and the Fulbright Foundation with both resources and encouragement. A number of colleagues across the campus, especially William Fowler from the History Department, have provided endless insight into the world of New England in the 19ᵗʰ century. It is nice to work at such a wonderful institution.

The Dorchester Historical Society (DHS) has also been enthusiastic about this project from the beginning. The Society has worked for many years to keep the memory of Edward Everett alive, and officials at the DHS envisioned this project as a vital continuation of their work. The Director of the DHS, Earl Taylor, smoothed the path at every stage of development, taking care of the details of publication and marketing in a timely and professional manner. Earl and the others dedicated to the preservation of the history of Dorchester are to be commended for their commitment to this book.

The present effort rests squarely on the shoulders of other scholars whose writings are cited throughout this text. The most comprehensive work on Everett's oratory comes from Ronald Reid. Starting with his dissertation in 1954 at Purdue University, Reid devoted his scholarly career to studying the rhetoric of Edward Everett. Most notable is Reid's 1990 book, *Edward Everett: Unionist Orator*, filled as it is with facts about Everett's oratorical career, and containing a chronology of religious, legislative, and demonstrative public orations given by Everett during his lifetime. Reid's chronology is an invaluable guide to Everett's oratorical career, and I am indebted to this now departed scholar.

Three Everett biographers must also be recognized. The first is Paul Revere Frothingham, whose *Edward Everett: Orator and Statesman*, written in 1925, is the only comprehensive biography of Everett's life. While Frothingham does not conduct rhetorical analyses of Everett's orations, he comments on many of them as a way of building human interest into this compelling American story.

Frothingham's work has been criticized for being at times romantic and at times apologetic; it is, nevertheless, an encyclopedic account of Everett's life, and it has served as a foundational text in the preparation of this book. Paul Varg's *Edward Everett: The Intellectual in the Turmoil of Politics*, written in 1992, is an analysis of the way in which Everett's conservatism and devotion to the preservation of the Union shaped and defined his politics. In this respect, Varg and Reid provide similar points of view from which to understand Everett's life and his oratory. Finally, Irving Bartlett's essay *Edward Everett Reconsidered*, published in the *New England Quarterly* in 1996, provides a much-needed revision of Edward Everett's life, especially his politics. Bartlett, while recognizing Everett's errors in judgment on the slavery issue, puts this matter into the broader context of Everett's life and career on the public stage and makes a persuasive argument for reassigning Everett a more favorable place in American history. At the time of his death, Bartlett was preparing to write a full biography of Everett, updating the Frothingham biography and adding new research to illuminate the life of this distinguished American. This book has benefited greatly from the work he had already completed.

The author is also indebted to those many devoted friends who eulogized Edward Everett upon his death and at memorial services for him in later years. Two names must be mentioned. The first is Elias Nason, whose eulogy in 1865, shortly after Everett's death, is a model of classical oratory. Nason's address imposes a *veil of silence* about some aspects of Everett's life; at the same time, his speech *is* Edward Everett, judging from all that we know about him. The other eulogy is the main oration presented at the centennial anniversary of the birth of Edward Everett in 1895 in Boston by the Reverend James DeNormandie. Realistic and frank with regard to Everett's failings, but adamant that Everett's life *was without soil and without suspicion,* the eulogy is often cited and often praised.

Finally, Edward Everett himself must be recognized for his own revealing thoughts about his oratory in his voluminous diary and in the preface to his two-volume work, *Everett's Orations and Speeches*, published in 1850. The book you are about to read is a humble attempt to add further to our knowledge of the life of Edward Everett, particularly his career as a public orator.

I have also had the support of friends, colleagues, and students at Northeastern University. First among these friends is Jim Cooke, the noted actor and interpreter of Everett and other great American historical figures such as John Quincy Adams, Daniel Webster, and Calvin Coolidge. In the midst of a busy career, Jim has read the manuscript, assuring the accuracy of the text and its readability. Jim has also allowed me full access to his books on Edward Everett; in fact, to his full collection of Everett memorabilia, and for this he has my undying gratitude.

Marilyn Root, graduate school colleague and former associate dean of the College of Communication at Boston University, provided numerous comments on the text early in its development. My close friend, the distinguished American diplomat Robert Tynes, also provided insightful suggestions to improve the manuscript. With financial support from the College of Arts and Sciences at Northeastern University, Alexandra Anweiler has worked as the research fellow on this project. She has provided invaluable assistance in the search for documents to support the ideas and opinions in this text. She has also provided editorial assistance throughout the drafting process. My hope is that Alexandra has learned from me a tiny fraction of what Edward Everett learned from his professor of rhetoric and oratory, John Quincy Adams.

Most importantly, I want to thank the editor of this book, Linda Smith Rhoads. Lynn's work as editor of the *New England Quarterly* gave her the broad perspective and the experience necessary to produce a final text that is written in a style accessible to the general public. While I take full responsibility for the contents of this book, my deepest appreciation is extended to Lynn.

Let us turn now to the world of Edward Everett to see why it is that I, and many others, have called him the greatest orator in American history.

—*Richard A. Katula*
Boston, 2008

Introduction

Edward Everett (1794–1865) was America's first Ph.D., a professor of Greek studies at Harvard University, a United States congressman, governor of Massachusetts, minister to England, president of Harvard University, secretary of state, United States senator, and vice-presidential candidate. In the course of this distinguished career, he was also the most celebrated orator of the nineteenth century, a time often referred to as the *Golden Age of American Oratory*. It was once said of Everett that *no occasion was complete without the grace and finish of his classical eloquence* (DeNormandie, p. 27). Most citizens in his day would have agreed, and yet in ours he is scarcely known.

Everett's oratory is intimately linked to the names of two other Americans, perhaps the country's greatest: George Washington and Abraham Lincoln. Washington's *Farewell Address* provided Everett with the main themes that infused his oratory; he repaid his hero by delivering his memorable speech *The Character of Washington* 137 times across the nation, earning $87,000 (a vast sum of money in 1860), which he contributed to the campaign to purchase Washington's home, Mount Vernon, so that it could be preserved as a national monument. Lincoln delivered his two-minute masterpiece the *Gettysburg Address* immediately after Everett presented his two-hour oration at the site of that epic Civil War battle. It is a sad fact, however, that whereas Washington and Lincoln remain iconic figures in American history—and justifiably so—Edward Everett, although celebrated and famous in his own day, is largely forgotten. This book seeks to redress that grievous error, revealing Edward Everett to be a brilliant, influential, and charismatic figure among that first generation of Americans to whom the national torch had been passed by the Founders. In particular, the book explores Everett's unsurpassed career as an orator, revealing how he achieved that status and presenting numerous examples of the soaring rhetoric with which he held his audiences spellbound over the course of forty years.

For those who do not know Everett, chapter 1 reviews his life and discusses four reasons why he has been relegated to second-tier status in American history: the lack of a comprehensive biography about him until 1925, his gradualist approach to the slavery issue, misconceptions surrounding his address at the dedication ceremony at Gettysburg on November 19, 1863, and his failure in the view of some to produce a *great* book.

Chapter 2 revisits *The Golden Age of American Oratory,* that period from approximately 1820 to 1920 when oratory served as the new nation's primary medium of communication, and when many public orators became celebrities, some as famous as any celebrity in America today. The chapter then turns to the education of those orators in the nineteenth century, in particular the education of Edward Everett. Everett gave his first speech at the age of three. During the next fourteen years, he mastered the *science* of rhetoric and the *art* of oratory with the aid of mentors like John Quincy Adams, the first Boylston Professor of Rhetoric and Oratory at Harvard University. Upon his graduation from Harvard in 1811, Edward Everett was fully prepared to become the nation's most illustrious public speaker, and as we shall see, he did.

Chapter 3 provides a rhetorical analysis of four of Everett's most notable orations: his momentous Phi Beta Kappa Society lecture, *The Circumstances Favorable to the Progress of Literature in America,* delivered in 1824 at Harvard University; his 1833 Fourth of July Oration, *The Seven Years War, The School of the Revolution,* presented in Worcester, Massachusetts; his moving eulogy on his mentor John Quincy Adams, delivered in Faneuil Hall, Boston, in 1848; and his most brilliant and successful oration *The Character of Washington,* performed across the country from 1856 through 1860. By looking at the four genres of oratory for which Everett was famous—lectures, festival orations, eulogies, and memorial addresses—we see him defining, idealizing, romanticizing, and memorializing his new and rising nation, America, while at the same time warning audiences of the perils of party faction and other threats to the nation's preservation.

Chapter 4 then turns to the speech that Everett believed was his crowning achievement, his Gettysburg address, declaimed at the dedication of America's first national cemetery on November 19, 1863, four months after the Battles of Gettysburg during America's Civil War on July 1, 2, and 3 of that year. Through an analysis of this speech, we learn why it was praised and why it was criticized; why it was discussed widely in Everett's day; and why it remains today the perfect complement to Lincoln's transformative *Gettysburg Address.*

Great orations in the nineteenth century are usually at the center of stories that are as entertaining and informative as the speeches themselves. Everett's speeches are no exception, surrounded as they are by compelling narratives that give us *snapshots in time* of a nation awakening to its destiny, struggling with its demons, celebrating its triumphs, and lamenting its failures. As America's premier public speaker, Everett reveals through his oratory the way that Americans of the time were addressed by the celebrated speakers of the day, and thus how they constructed their culture word by word.

Throughout this journey, we will witness how the classical ages of Greece and Rome transformed American culture in the nineteenth century. The Greek Revival period, from approximately 1820 to 1870, provided the cultural subtext upon which America's intellectuals drew to construct the nation's identity and to set its course for generations to come. We see how Edward Everett, as one of the pioneers of the classical revival, became the quintessential statesmen of the new America, its most public voice, and its herald to the world.

WORKS CITED

DeNormandie, James. *Oration*, Centennial Anniversary of the Birth of EdwardEverett. The Dorchester Historical Society. Boston: Rockwell and Churchill, City Printers. 1895.

Edward Everett:
an American life

EVENT/LOCATION	NOTABLE ADDRESSES* AND ACCOMPLISHMENTS
April 11, 1794 Born, Dorchester, Mass.	
1803 Attends private schools in Boston	
1807–1811 Attends Harvard University	Class Valedictorian
February 9, 1814 Ordained Pastor, Brattle Street Church, Boston, Mass.	Delivers 80 original sermons, repeated upon request.
1815 Boston, Mass.	Book: *In Defense of Christianity*

EVENT/LOCATION	NOTABLE ADDRESSES* AND ACCOMPLISHMENTS
1815–1825 Professor of Greek Language and Literature, Harvard University, Cambridge, Mass.	Leading figure in Greek Revival Movement, 1820–1870. Appeals for American government to support Greek War of Independence.
Summer, April 1815 Studies in Germany; earns Ph.D. in Classics, Gottingen University, 1817	First American to earn Ph.D.
1820–1824 Editor, *North American Review*	Author of 118 essays, 61 as editor
May 8, 1822 Boston, Mass.	Marries Charlotte Brooks
August 26, 1824 Phi Beta Kappa Oration, Harvard University, Cambridge, Mass.	*The Circumstances Favorable to the Progress of Literature in America*
January 1825–March 1835 Congressman, U.S. House of Representatives	Remarks about slavery in Debut speech, March 25, 1825
July 4, 1833 Worcester, Mass.	*The Seven Years War, The School of the Revolution*

EVENT/LOCATION	NOTABLE ADDRESSES* AND ACCOMPLISHMENTS
1835–1839 Governor of Massachusetts	
1841–1845 U.S. Minister to England	
1846–1848 President, Harvard University	Inaugural Address, April 30, 1846
April 15, 1848 Boston, Mass.	*Eulogy on John Quincy Adams*
1852–1853 Secretary of State, Fillmore Administration	
1853–1854 U.S. Senator, Massachusetts	
1856–1860 Cities and towns across the United States	*The Character of Washington.* repeated 137 times
Autumn 1858 New York, *New York Ledger*	58 essays on Washington and other subjects. Later published as *The Washington Papers.*
1860 Candidate for Vice-President	Constitutional-Union ticket

EVENT/LOCATION	NOTABLE ADDRESSES* AND ACCOMPLISHMENTS
November 19, 1863 Gettysburg, Pennsylvania	*Oration at the Commemoration of the National Cemetery at Gettysburg*
January 15, 1865 Died in Boston, Mass. Interment in Mount Auburn Cemetery, Cambridge, Mass.	

*Everett delivered numerous other addresses, especially while governor of Massachusetts. The chronology here lists some of his most important lectures, eulogies, and ceremonial orations. For a complete list of Everett's public addresses see Appendix A.

Edward Everett
1860

1

Edward Everett: *A Full Life, Well Lived*

Assuredly no grander subject is likely to be offered to the poet, the painter, the writer, or the orator, for many a long year to come, than the life, career, and character of Edward Everett.
—*Winslow Lewis*, 1865

REMEMBERING EDWARD EVERETT

The ancient Greek dramatist Euripedes writes, *When good men die their goodness does not perish, but lives though they are gone.* Here is one of the most hopeful truisms of the classical age. It is true, however, only when succeeding generations take measures to preserve that good. Otherwise, as Shakespeare reminds us in Marc Antony's eulogy to Caesar, *The evil men do lives after them; the good is oft interred with their bones.* No American of the nineteenth century devoted more of his energy to memorializing the deeds of others—to preserving their goodness—than Edward Everett. He lived his life in the spirit of Euripedes.

Towns, schools, and village squares have been dedicated to the memory of Edward Everett. His name is engraved in the façade of the Boston Public Library. Notable Americans such as the minister Edward Everett Hale and the actor Edward Everett Horton remind us of the many parents who hoped their children would achieve the same success as their namesake. A small library of books and scholarly essays has reflected on the life and career of Edward Everett. And on appropriate occasions, his friends and family have memorialized him in speeches. The illustrious Roman statesman Cicero thought that to be remembered in some epic sense was the most fitting reward of a life well lived. Edward Everett has certainly been thus rewarded.

And deservedly so. As the chronology suggests, he was a man of enormous accomplishment, selflessly serving throughout his life his community, his state, the country, and the cause of the liberal arts and sciences. But a chronology can tell only so much. It is through the details of his life story that we come to know Everett more intimately, and through an analysis of his oratory—his most permanent mark on American history—that we come to engage with him as young America's most compelling public speaker. For those not yet acquainted with Edward Everett, other than perhaps as the *other* voice at Gettysburg, the details of his life will be revealed throughout this volume as they augment and illuminate my primary focus, his oratory. For now, we sketch those events with the broad strokes necessary to lay the foundation for our review of his eloquence.

Edward Everett was born in Dorchester, Massachusetts, to Oliver and Lucy Hill Everett, on April 11, 1794, the fourth child in a family of eight children, six boys and two girls. Edward distinguished himself early as a brilliant student with a prodigious memory, and he entered Harvard University at the age of thirteen, graduating four years later as class valedictorian. During his years at Harvard, he excelled in every subject, but had a particular fondness for philosophy and rhetoric, to both of which he devoted endless hours of study, often illuminated by only the *midnight oil*. One of his most vivid recollections of those student days comes from his class in metaphysics, in particular the study of John Locke's *Essay Concerning Human Understanding*:

> *We recited from it three times a day, the four first days of the*
> *week, the recitation of Thursday afternoon, being a review of*

the rest. We were expected to give the substance of the author's remarks, but were at liberty to condense them and to use our own words.... I had at that time a memory which recoiled from nothing, and I soon found that the shortest process was to learn the text by heart nearly verbatim. I recollect particularly on one occasion of the review on Thursday afternoon, that I was called upon to recite early and I went on repeating word for word, and paragraph for paragraph, and finally, not being stopped by our pleased tutor, page after page, till I finally went through in that way the greater part of the eleven recitations of the week. (Frothingham, p. 13)

Little wonder was it, then, that Everett's classmates, all older, referred to the studious young man as *Edward Ever-at-It* or that the faculty, including the president of the university, John T. Kirkland, and the distinguished Boston minister Joseph Buckminster, noticed immediately that they had someone quite special in their midst.

Upon Everett's graduation from Harvard in 1811, Kirkland and Buckminster convinced him to study for the ministry, a task to which he obediently committed himself and for which he earned his Master of Arts degree in 1813. Even though fortune would eventually turn him away from the ministry, he remained a devoutly religious person throughout his life, deeply influenced by his belief in Christian doctrine.

When Buckminster died unexpectedly in 1812, the pew proprietors of what was then the most prestigious church in Boston, the Brattle Street Church, drafted young Edward to *supply* the congregation with sermons, as they put it, *for a while* and thereafter to assume the weighty duties full time. With some hesitation the now nineteen-year-old accepted, and for the next year and a half he delivered weekly sermons that filled the church pews, and even the church windows, with souls eager for his jeremiads. The substance of his sermons centered on the often paradoxical messages present in biblical text, toward which he would take an *antisagogic*, or balanced, approach. This two-sided mode of analysis was of great assistance to Everett's listeners, enmeshed as they were in an age of rationalism and seeking to reconcile their new age with the traditional biblical teachings of their Puritan forebears. For Everett, the antisagogic approach allowed him to explicate a text without taking sides on its application (Reid, 1990, p. 18).

Birthplace of Edward Everett
Dorchester, Massachusetts

While the content of his preaching was noticeably more expository than exhortative, Everett's speaking style was described by some as *florid and fancy*, leading one critic to notice in his sermons *more of the flowers of rhetoric than the fruits of the gospel* (Varg, p. 18). Others, however, thought his manner engaging, and Paul Revere Frothingham, Everett's early-twentieth-century biographer, records that,

> *He abounded in splendid allusions, in quotations impossible to forget, in daring imagery, in parable…. All his speech was music, and with such variety and invention that the ear was never tired.* (Frothingham, p. 25)

However one judged the young minister's substance or his style, all soon noticed that Edward Everett was a unique orator, *stately* being the word that came closest to describing him. In his Memoir of Ralph Waldo Emerson, James Elliot Cabot notes that the Concord sage and his brother Edward looked eagerly forward to each Everett sermon and would learn by heart *certain of his striking sayings* (Frothingham, p. 25). At one point, Emerson remarked in his diary that *Nature finished this man. He seems perfectly built, perfectly sound and whole; his eye, voice, hand, exactly obey his thought* (Varg, p. 129).

Despite Everett's success in the pulpit, his ministry exhausted him. In addition to his weekly sermons at the Brattle Street Church, he was frequently invited to deliver them to other congregations in the Boston area, which he politely agreed to do amidst the many other duties attendant upon a pastor devoted to his flock. More to the point, however, Everett grew tired of the intellectual constraints of interpreting passages from the Bible and the impossible task imposed upon one so young to advise others, mostly his seniors, in Christian morality. In 1815, Everett abruptly resigned his appointment.

Just as quickly, he accepted the post of professor of Greek studies at Harvard, this at the youthful age of twenty-one. The position brought with it a large grant to study abroad, so that same year, prior to his actually teaching, he began a four-year course of study in Germany, where he discovered German romanticism, immersed himself in classical philosophy, and mingled with many of Europe's most celebrated intellectuals and literary figures. Upon his return in 1819, having become America's first Ph.D. recipient (Göttingen University, 1817), he assumed the teaching duties attendant to his professorship. At Harvard, he taught future intellectual giants such as Emerson, and he became a seminal figure in the Greek Revival movement, that, as dramatically as the Revolution had defined American politics, was now defining American culture.

While a student in Europe, Everett had traveled to Greece where he ascended the acropolis in Athens to marvel at the Parthenon. He had walked the battlefields—Marathon, Salamis, Plataea—that had witnessed the bloody birth of Western civilization, and he had stood on the hill of the Pnyx from which Pericles addressed the citizens of Athens once each week during the world's first experiment in direct democracy. Everett was inspired. Greece, he came to believe, was the perfect model for a new nation searching for its own identity. Upon returning to America, he found that other intellectuals were equally eager to break with the past and embrace the very classicism of which Everett was the nation's premier scholar. As Talbot Hamlin, a scholar of the Greek Revival, notes,

> *All through New England this new yeast was working—the leaven of individualism, of personal assertion, of freedom inspired by European romanticism and growing cosmopolitan contacts. And the first product of this swift fermentation was classicism—a new and vivid feeling of the reality and beauty of Greece and Rome. It was as though Greek culture and Roman culture had suddenly become symbols of all that was free, refined, thoughtful, and—especially—beautiful in human life.* (p. 97)

Everett was in the vanguard of this dramatic cultural awakening, and for the next forty years he would bring the ideals of the classical world to the American public through his essays and, most notably, his oratory.

Unique among his contemporaries, Everett possessed an enlightened, prismatic perspective. Out of his European experiences had emerged a transcendent view of America as a millennial nation. His vision soared beyond America's Puritan origins, its Revolutionary struggle for independence, and its sentimental attachments to *old Europe*. This idea of a uniquely American culture, emerging out of these many influences but now free to develop its own traditions, was one that would, in both the brightest and the darkest moments of his life, suffuse Everett's rhetoric.

The years of teaching at Harvard were among Everett's most successful and productive. His students included the brilliant young minds of the day, most born in America and all eager to embrace his classical view of the world. His star pupil and ardent admirer, Ralph Waldo Emerson, would go on to develop Everett's teachings into the first purely American intellectual movement, transcendentalism. It was also during this period that Everett married Charlotte Brooks (May 8, 1822), whom he called *Charlie*; their marriage was long and happy.

During his Harvard tenure, Everett was appointed editor of the North American Review, a literary journal that he would refashion into one of the nineteenth century's seminal intellectual publications. He wrote 118 essays for the Review (61 while serving as editor), and edited hundreds of others on every imaginable topic in poetry, literature, politics, trade, and even business. The North American Review was soon acclaimed throughout America and Europe, presaging in its essays the transcendentalist movement and, more grandly, a uniquely American tradition in the arts, sciences, and literature. Subscriptions increased from 500 to, by the close of Everett's term as editor in 1824, 3,000. He became known throughout America and Europe as an intellectual force for progress in the liberal pursuits of the mind. He would reinforce this reputation in his first major public address, entitled *The Circumstances Favorable to the Progress of Literature in America*, the Phi Beta Kappa Society lecture that he delivered at Harvard University in 1824. We will review this transformational lecture in detail in chapter 3.

The Phi Beta Kappa Society oration was a national sensation, and its triumph swept Everett into politics. In 1826, Massachusetts sent him to the United States Congress, and for the next ten years he engaged in the era's most contentious political debates, especially those regarding slavery, the issue that would eventually divide

America and drive it to civil war. Slavery was also the issue on which Everett would stumble badly in one of his first speeches on the House floor, and this mistake would shadow him, as we shall see, for the rest of his life.

In 1835 Everett was elected governor of Massachusetts. For the next four years, he led the citizenry of the commonwealth in a lively and progressive agenda, including establishing the nation's first public school system in 1838 and the first teacher training institutes, or *normal* schools, as well as sponsoring humane prison reform and other initiatives that aided the development of agriculture, science, and business. In 1840, after losing his reelection bid by one vote, (because so many citizens — even his closest friends — thought him a shoo-in for reelection), a shocked and dispirited Everett retired briefly to private life.

President John Tyler recognized Everett's reputation as a devoted public servant, and the next year, in 1841, he appointed Everett to the post of minister to England, the official title of which was Envoy Extraordinary and Minister Plenipotentiary of the United States at the Court of Great Britain, London. His years as a diplomat in Europe were among his happiest. Having been nurtured on German philosophy, French art, and English literature, Everett was at ease in the Old World elegance of England, and the English royalty and aristocracy were equally comfortable with him. He is responsible, in part, for establishing the close relationship that has existed between America and Great Britain for the past 170 years. In particular, he led the negotiations to establish the northeast boundary between the United States and Canada and to secure for American fishermen the right to fish the Bay of Fundy in perpetuity. Knotty issues at the time, these matters required skillful diplomacy based on a carefully built trust between the parties involved. Everett's unimpeachable integrity was critical to the peaceful resolution of these and other concerns that constituted the life of a foreign minister in the mid-nineteenth century.

When Tyler's term as president ended, Everett was recalled from his post in England. He was quickly drafted to become president of Harvard University, a position he reluctantly accepted in 1846 and in which he served until his resignation in December 1848. In his inaugural address, Everett made it clear that learning was but a barren pursuit if not governed by moral principle:

> *We have thus far considered a liberal education as designed, in the first place, to furnish an ample store of useful knowledge by way of preparation for the duties of life; and secondly, as intended to unfold and exercise the mental powers. But these objects, important as they certainly are, and fitting in their attainment too often the highest ambition of parents and children, are in reality of but little worth if unaccompanied by the most precious endowment of our fallen nature, a pure and generous spirit, warmed by kind affections, governed by moral principle, and habitually influenced by motives and hopes that look forward into eternity.* (Frothingham, p. 274)

In his effort to activate these principles of learning, Everett reintroduced mandatory chapel attendance for students, and he *encouraged* it for the faculty. He served as an example to everyone on campus by living the words in his inaugural address. President Everett quickly discovered, however, that the majority of students had subordinated academic life to the more reckless pursuit of mischief. Following his core principles, the chief academic officer of the distinguished academic institution found himself little more than the disciplinarian of a band of wealthy malcontents. He spent his days dealing with petty matters such as absence from lectures, disorderly conduct, and drunkenness. When not enmeshed in such trivial affairs, he was addressing more serious, and sometimes criminal, student offenses: exploding toilets with vials of gunpowder, procuring the services of prostitutes, and setting the roofs of university buildings ablaze.

One incident during his tenure deserves special mention for it speaks to Everett's character. A young black man named Beverly Williams sought to take the examinations for admission to the university. Everett knew Williams as a scholar and tutor to one of his sons. A rumor was started that even if Williams should pass the entrance exams, he would not be admitted. Everett put this rumor to rest with the following words:

> *The admission to Harvard College depends upon examinations: and if this boy passes the examinations, he will be admitted; and if the white students choose to withdraw, all the income of the College will be devoted to his education.*
> (Frothingham, p. 299)

Everett's legacy as president of Harvard is mixed. As a renowned scholar who possessed a gentle nature, he was temperamentally ill suited for the duties he found himself performing. But through all of it, he remained devoted to the task of reforming this illustrious American university. Even though he found most days unbearable and exhausting, he awoke ready to serve on each. The faculty of the College made this clear in the letter they sent to him upon his resignation:

> *We deem it proper at such a time to express to you our sense of the value of your services to the Institution during the three years of your administration. We have seen in our course an unsurpassed fidelity in discharging the duties of the office, always laborious and often painful; and we have appreciated the spirit of self-sacrifice with which you have consecrated your time, your thoughts, your energies, to the intellectual and moral progress of the young men.*
> (Frothingham, p. 296)

For three years, and while maintaining his permanent residence in Boston, Everett retired to a rented home in Cambridge. He intended to write a book on the modern law of nations, and he worked on a compilation of Daniel Webster's speeches. The book was not to be, however, as in 1852, President Millard Fillmore appointed him secretary of state. After just a year in the post, the citizens of Massachusetts elected him to complete the Senate term of Daniel Webster, who had died that October. Even though Everett would leave a legacy, albeit brief, of accomplishment and dedication to his nation and the cause of preserving the Union, he quickly grew weary of the jangling discord in the halls of Congress. Never one to enjoy the rough-and-tumble world of politics, he saw in the debates about slavery the defeat of civil negotiation and a victory for sectional factionalism, the very polarization of interests about which his hero, George Washington, had warned the nation in his *Farewell Address* of 1799. His spirit broken, his hopes for America dashed on the rocks of faction, and his health suffering, Everett resigned from the Senate in 1854, returning home to his beloved wife, Charlotte, and their family.

Between 1854 and 1860, Everett's fame as an orator grew to legendary status. In two nationwide tours, he delivered his magnum opus *The Character of Washington* to sold-out audiences. He also presented his brilliant oration *Franklin, the Boston Boy* to equally enthusiastic crowds up and down the Atlantic coast. We will return to *The Character of Washington* in chapter 3, for it remains today a remarkable speech garbed in an unforgettable story.

As the Civil War approached in 1860, Everett was persuaded to run for vice president of the United States on the Constitutional-Union ticket, an aggregation of politicians devoted to saving the Union through a benign approach to the slavery issue. It was an awkward and ill-considered decision, and Everett, while opposed to Abraham Lincoln during the presidential campaign, offered his support as soon as Lincoln was elected. Everett served the beleaguered president throughout the Civil War, often as a behind-the-scenes advisor on securing England's support for the North.

In public, Everett spent the first two years of the conflict delivering his speech *Causes and Conduct of the War*. Now an older man approaching seventy, Everett delivered the address sixty times throughout the Northern states. He blamed the war on Southern radicals, convinced his audience to support the president, and raised untold sums of money to support the soldiers in the field. And, of course, he presented the most memorable speech of his career at the dedication of the cemetery in Gettysburg, Pennsylvania. We shall review this historical event and Everett's speech in chapter 4.

As the war was winding down, Everett contracted a disease, probably pneumonia, and died at his home in Boston on January 15, 1865. Throughout his life, Edward Everett preached that America was a unique place with endless possibilities. He dreaded war. He believed in the power of words to resolve even the thorniest of issues, and to bind the Union together. From these values he never wavered, and they would become the central themes of his oratory during his later years. His principles drew him toward a conservative political view, an enduring faith in America, and a patriotism born out of dedication to his God and his country.

Well liked throughout his life, Everett was kind, gentle, diffident, engaging, and sophisticated. He was not often jovial nor was he universally approachable. As his son William Everett once put it, his father

> *did not hold that every introduction was a passport to intimacy nor confound acquaintance, friends and kindred spirits all equally in a tumultuous good fellowship.*
> (Bartlett, p. 458)

His letters and diary, however, reveal a devoted husband and father, and a man who, even during his most painful experiences such as his Harvard presidency, was a gentleman to all. One thing was obvious to everyone: he was always the smartest person in the room. During his lifetime, he was a celebrated intellectual whom princes and presidents sought out for advice, a famous speaker whose eloquence drew throngs, and a man widely recognized for his integrity and his prescience in this age of awakening.

EDWARD EVERETT'S PLACE IN HISTORY
And yet, although renowned in his time, Edward Everett is largely forgotten today, remembered if at all as the man who spoke for two hours before President Abraham Lincoln delivered his legendary *Gettysburg Address*. It is reasonable to ask why so illustrious a life as Edward Everett's has been consigned to history's back shelf. Four reasons suggest themselves.

First, William Everett, Edward's son, failed in his promise to write a biography of his father (Orations, 1892, vol. 4, preface). His neglect pained and embarrassed him throughout his life, and he tired of being hounded to complete a task that was simply beyond his powers of perseverance. And, since William carefully controlled his father's papers, it was not until 1925 that Paul Revere Frothingham published his comprehensive biography of Edward Everett. But by then, as one Everett admirer predicted, *The desire for it [had] died away* (Frothingham, p. ix).

Second, though he was opposed to slavery and thought it a consummate evil, Everett was reluctant to speak out on the key issue of the day; when he finally did so, he made a political and personal disaster of it. Northern newspapers and leading abolitionists publicly condemned him for failing to support the abolitionist crusade and for his rare but sometimes troubling pronouncements about the status of American slavery. This one issue would be writ large in his legacy, prompting one notable speaker, the Reverend James DeNormandie, to remark on the centennial celebration of Everett's birth that,

> *There were many things in that great conflict hard for*
> *friends of the anti-slavery cause ever to forget, in the*
> *calculating silence of so many men eminent in gifts*
> *and in station.* (DeNormandie, p. 17)

Third, Edward Everett's most supreme oratorical achievement, his remarkable two-hour address at the dedication of America's first national cemetery at Gettysburg, was overshadowed by Abraham Lincoln's two-minute masterpiece in which, as historian Irving Bartlett has noted, the president

> *articulated an emerging American identity that most of his*
> *audience could not grasp at first hearing but which later gen-*
> *erations would instinctively understand as the classic answer*
> *to the question that had nagged the country for years: "What*
> *does it mean to be an American?"* (Bartlett, p. 458).

There is a fourth reason for Everett's second-tier status in American history. As a child prodigy gifted with a giant intellect and a memory that, as he said, *recoiled from nothing* and as the first American to earn a Ph.D., it was expected of him that he would write a great book, or at least that he would apply the genius endowed to him by Providence to matters of an intellectual cast. The leading scholars of his day assumed that he would become a man of letters, as Emerson had become, rather than a mere politician, or simply a *popular festival orator,* as his brother-in-law Charles Francis Adams Jr. once referred to him.

The latter three deficiencies of which Everett has been accused are of significant import, and each requires some explanation early in this journey through his distinguished oratorical career.

On the matter of slavery, Everett made one speech on the floor of the House during his first term in Congress. It was an ill-considered, three-hour address given by a man temperamentally ill suited for the polemics of legislative debate. It was also a speech that would haunt him for the rest of his life.

The speech, only Everett's second delivered to the entire body, was in response to a resolution offered by a Mr. McDuffie of South Carolina that would have amended the Constitution to prohibit contested Presidential elections (such as the previous election of John Quincy Adams in 1824) from devolving to the House of Representatives. The debate became contentious, lasting three weeks and carried out among the entire assemblage (rather than in committee). As with most matters before Congress in the 1820s, the subtext of the debate was slavery whereas the ostensible matter before the body was the wisdom of amending the Constitution. Everett's interest was primarily centered on the latter for he was, from his earliest youth, passionately devoted to the preservation of the Union through adherence to the rule of law as ratified in the Constitution. Whatever his intentions may have been (perhaps his natural tendency to be conciliatory), his remarks at one critical juncture during the speech grew gratuitous toward his Southern colleagues, and in a moment of digression he turned, regrettably, to the issue of slavery:

> *I ought, perhaps, to add that if there are any members of
> this House of that class of politicians to whom the gentleman
> from North Carolina (Mr. Sanders) alluded, as having the
> disposition, though not the power, to disturb the compromise
> in the Constitution on this point [slavery], I am not of the
> number. Neither am I one of those citizens of the North, to
> whom another honorable gentleman lately referred, in a
> publication to which his name was subscribed, who would
> think it immoral and irreligious to join in putting down a
> servile insurrection at the South. I am no soldier, Sir; my
> habits and education are very unmilitary; but there is no
> cause in which I would sooner buckle a knapsack to my back,
> and put a musket on my shoulder than that. I would cede the
> whole continent to any one who would take it—to England,
> to France, to Spain; I would see it sunk in the bottom of the
> ocean, before I would see any part of this fair America con-
> verted into a continental Hayti [sic], by that awful process of
> bloodshed and desolation by which alone such a catastrophe
> could be brought on.* (Frothingham, p. 105)

Worse, despite noting that slavery was a beneficent institution to
neither the slave nor the slaveowner, Everett went on to apply biblical
evidence to the matter:

> *I cannot admit that religion has but one voice to the slave,
> and that this voice is, "Rise against your master." No, Sir,
> the New Testament says, "Slaves, obey your masters"; and
> though I know full well that, in the benignant operation of
> Christianity which gathered master and slave around the
> same communion table, this unfortunate institution disap-
> peared in Europe; yet I cannot admit that, while it subsists,
> and where it subsists, its duties are not presupposed and
> sanctified by religion.* (Frothingham, p. 105)

The following day, Everett was pained to read his own words, and
abolitionists such as Wendell Phillips immediately attacked him.

The freshman congressman was condemned in the Northern press and rebuked by political and religious leaders, many of whom were admirers of the erudite minister–turned–politician. The most biting comment came from a New York clergyman who wrote to Everett that opposition to slavery was a question of rights and decency, whereas the preservation of the Union was a question of politics and expediency (Varg, p. 186). The Reverend James DeNormandie, in his eulogy to Everett in 1895, would put history's fine point on the matter: *When you are in doubt in the great game of life, over any moral question, PLAY THE CARD OF HUMAN LIBERTY* (p. 17).

Everett made a similarly unnecessary statement about slavery in his gubernatorial inaugural in 1836. In general, however, he chose to remain silent or diffident about the greatest issue facing his generation even though he strongly believed that slavery was a *great evil.*

This sense of diffidence born out of the contradiction between his personal views about slavery and the devotion to the preservation of the Union that formed the core of his political beliefs is no more clearly represented than in a speech Everett delivered on the floor of the United States Senate on February 7, 1854, during the debate on the Missouri Compromise:

> *I believe the Union of these States is the greatest possible blessing – that it comprises within itself all other blessings, political, natural, and social; and I trust that my own eyes may close long before the day shall come – if it ever shall come – when that Union shall be at an end. Sir, I share the opinions and the sentiments of that part of the country where I was born and educated, where my ashes will be laid, and where my children will succeed me! But in relation to my fellow-citizens in other parts of the country, I will treat their constitutional and their legal rights with respect, and their feelings with tenderness. I believe them to be as good Christians, as good patriots, as good men as we are. And I claim that we, in our turn, are as good as they. I rejoiced to hear my friend from Kentucky utter the opinion that a wise and gracious Providence, in His own good time, will find the ways and the*

> *channels to remove from the land what I consider this great*
> *evil, and I do not expect that what has been done in three*
> *centuries and a half is to be undone in a day, or a year, or a*
> *few years; and I believe that in the meantime the desired end*
> *will be retarded rather than promoted by passionate, sectional*
> *irritation.... And finally, I doubt not that in His own*
> *good time the Ruler of all will vindicate the most glorious*
> *of his prerogatives, "from seeming evil, still seducing good."*
> (Frothingham, p.349)

The speech was received with favor by both Northern and
Southern Senators, most of whom by this time understood the famed
Edward Everett to be a minister somewhat awkwardly disguised
as a politician. And there were other comments, some private and
some public, but all fell short of what the era demanded, especially
in Massachusetts. Charles Henry Dana, an Everett contemporary,
explains Everett's attitude toward slavery by noting that the value
Everett placed on the Union was

> *a solemn conviction that it was the one experiment, in the*
> *fullness of time, and under the most favorable circumstances*
> *possible, for the widest and highest moral and intellectual*
> *development of human nature.* (Varg, p.194)

Nevertheless, Everett's public timidity on the issue of slavery is no
trifling matter, and it cannot be blinked away or ignored. It is, in fair-
ness to him, the same reluctance felt by many Northern leaders of the
day, including Emerson and Lincoln himself, who condemned slavery
but who worried that any solution (especially abolition) to the slavery
problem short of one negotiated by both factions would end in war
and would split the country across its midsection from the east coast
to the west. Lincoln, who made his position clear on many occasions,
was most explicit in his First Inaugural Address:

> *Apprehension seems to exist among the people of the Southern*
> *States, that by the accession of a Republican Administration,*

> *their property, and their peace, and personal security, are to*
> *be endangered. There has never been any reasonable cause*
> *for such apprehension. Indeed, the most ample evidence to*
> *the contrary has all the while existed, and been open to their*
> *inspection. It is found in nearly all the published speeches of*
> *him who now addresses you. I do but quote from one of those*
> *speeches when I declare that "I have no purpose, directly or*
> *indirectly, to interfere with the institution of slavery in the*
> *States where it exists. I believe I have no lawful right to do so,*
> *and I have no inclination to do so."*
> (American Orators, Part 3, vol. 8, pp. 131–32)

Diffidence also characterized the views of many of the South's leading citizens. Robert E. Lee, who agonized about going to war over
slavery, made one contradictory public statement after another on the
issue, condemning radical voices in both the South and the North.
Elizabeth Brown Pryor notes that for Lee "There was no clear path
to rectitude—every avenue was strewn with irreconcilable principles"
(p. 23). Lee's resignation from the United States Army haunted him
for the rest of his life, and it divided his own family, as it did the entire
state of Virginia.

The Emancipation Proclamation, the Gettysburg Address, and
his Second Inaugural Address restored Lincoln's legacy. As for Lee,
although he was troubled throughout the conflict by competing loyal-
ties, was ennobled by defeat. As Pryor notes,

> *Lee's dilemma was not simply an historic wrestling match*
> *between patriotism and treachery. It stands as a critical*
> *moment in our nation's pageant because it forces us to con-*
> *sider some very basic questions: What is patriotism? What*
> *commands our first loyalty? Can loyalty be divided and still*
> *be true? It is the excruciating gray area that makes these*
> *questions universal. Lee tells us that the answer to each is*
> *highly subjective, but that each must be faced at the moment*
> *an individual is summoned, no matter how unsure and*
> *unprepared. And then his decision tells us something more:*

> *that following the heart's truth may lead to censure, or ago-*
> *nizing defeat—and yet be honored in itself.* (p. 21)

Like these men, and millions of other Americans, Edward Everett lived the very contradiction that had gnawed at the nation's conscience since the ratification of the Constitution. For example, he privately condemned the Compromise of 1850, including its Fugitive Slave Law, confiding to his friend Robert Winthrop that he would not himself return a fugitive to slavery even though it meant breaking the law. At the same time, however, he publicly absented himself from a Whig Party convention that would pass measures to condemn that very law (Varg, p. 162). His dilemma, then, was not his alone but that of his age. History would judge him wrong on the slavery matter, and he would admit as much during his oration at Gettysburg, but for this mistake in judgment, Edward Everett would pay history's price. Everett's legacy has also been tarnished by misconceptions surrounding his Gettysburg speech. The first myth is that it was too long. For instance, Noah Brooks, one of Lincoln's advisors, saw the printed version of Everett's speech a few days before the ceremony and warned the president of its length. But Lincoln chuckled at Brooks' remark knowing that it was customary for the main orator at an event of such historic proportions to speak for a long period of time. In fact, Lincoln himself noted in a letter to Everett following the ceremonies at Gettysburg that

> *In our respective parts yesterday you could not have been*
> *excused to make a short address, nor I a long one. I am*
> *pleased to know that, in your judgment, the little I did say*
> *was not entirely a failure. Of course, I knew Mr. Everett*
> *would not fail; and yet, while the whole discourse was emi-*
> *nently satisfactory, and will be of great value, there were*
> *passages in it that transcended my expectations.* (Edward
> Everett at Gettysburg, p. 15)

The sad reality for Everett's legacy is that Lincoln's speech is just the right length for modern anthologies, and it was short enough to be engraved on his memorial in Washington, D.C., while Everett's is too long for the attention span of most modern readers. Nevertheless, historians and critics alike now generally agree that both speakers delivered addresses of appropriate length on that historic occasion. The second myth surrounding the Gettysburg speech is that it was not successful. In fact, it was. The audience listened intently to the address, and when Everett returned to his seat just to the right of Lincoln, the president pressed his hand and said to him, *I am more than gratified; I am grateful to you, sir* (Everett, Papers, vol. 40, p. 182). With Everett's approval, the speech was immediately published in pamphlet form by the dedication's organizers and distributed for recruitment purposes across the Northern states; its proceeds were donated to a monument to the soldiers who died at Gettysburg (Everett, Papers, vol. 182, Reel 40). It was Garry Wills who restored Everett's address to an honored place in modern elocution when he noted that *Everett's classicism was as much the forerunner of Lincoln's talk as its foil or contrast* (p. 47). We shall develop this assertion in chapter 4.

A lesser but nevertheless enduring criticism of Everett's life is that he squandered his genius on the lecture circuit rather than devoting it to the great philosophical movements of his day, those to which he had been exposed during his education in Germany. This criticism is most evident in Emerson's Journal entry of May 1, 1846, the day following Everett's installation as president of Harvard University:

> *I was at Cambridge yesterday to see Everett inaugurated. His political brothers came as if to bring him to the convent door, and to grace with a sort of bitter courtesy his taking of the cowl. It is like the marriage of a girl; not until the wedding and the departure with her husband does it appear that she has actually and finally changed homes and connections and social caste. Webster I could so willingly have spared on this occasion. Everett was entitled to the entire field: and Webster came, who is his evil genius, and has done him incalculable harm by Everett's too much admiration of his iron nature; warped him from his true bias all these twenty years, and sent him cloud-hunting at Washington and London, to*

> *the ruin of all solid scholarship, and fatal diversion from the*
> *pursuit of his right prizes. It is in vain that Everett makes*
> *all these allusions to his public employments: he would fain*
> *deceive me and himself: he has never done anything therein,*
> *but has been, with whatever praises and titles and votes, a*
> *mere dangler and ornamental person.*
>
> (Frothingham, p. 272)

Was criticism such as Emerson's fair? Was it accurate? Everett himself was troubled enough by remarks about his choice of career to make a subtle reference to it in the preface to the first volume of his Orations and Speeches:

> *Some indulgence is perhaps due to these volumes for other*
> *reasons. With the exception of the lectures, the addresses*
> *contained in them were either written to be spoken, or hav-*
> *ing been spoken generally from heads prepared beforehand,*
> *were afterwards written out from the reporter's notes. The*
> *occasions, without exception, were of a popular character. It*
> *would be trying performances of this kind by a severe stan-*
> *dard, to expect of them the terseness and condensation which*
> *belongs to the writings of a more serious cast, prepared for*
> *the graver business occasions of life. (p. viii)*

Others who have weighed in on Everett's choice of vocation have defended him. At the 1894 centennial in his honor, for example, the aforementioned Reverend DeNormandie, while critical of some other aspects of Everett's life, addressed the matter of his choice of careers this way:

> *When he left the ministry for literature, there was great*
> *surprise and regret, still more was he found fault with for*
> *exchanging the peaceful kingdom of letters for the noisy*
> *arena of politics, or as one of his critics said, "that a gem*
> *of such rare water, should be so unprofitably set." I do not*
> *share this feeling in the least. I am not at all surprised at*

> *the fascination of politics over so many minds, and surely we*
> *see today as never before, that there is for us no security and*
> *no progress until those of the finest gifts, and the best culture,*
> *and the highest purpose, enter that sphere.* (p. 27)

Everett scholars generally agree with DeNormandie. Paul Varg, for
example, claims that as essayist and editor of the North American
Review, Everett was prescient in foreshadowing America's first great
intellectual movement, transcendentalism.

> *The North American Review became the first and leading*
> *journal of the day.... It offered new horizons that were*
> *refreshing. In this respect, it was a precursor of Emerson*
> *and the Transcendentalist movement. A highly respected*
> *scholar, Harry Hayden Clark, a historian of American*
> *literature, concluded that Emerson "could have found practi-*
> *cally all of his early transcendentalist and romantic ideas in*
> *the pages of the Review."* (Varg, p. 27)

Everett's essays were immensely popular among readers throughout America and Europe, and they ranged widely across the spectrum
of issues that faced the new nation: tariffs, free trade, education in
Europe, literature in America, ancient Greece, and the art of poetry. In
1915, at the centennial celebration of the Review, the unnamed historian of the event wrote that,

> *Mr. Everett closed his labors as editor with a contribution of*
> *a remarkable article on European politics which not another*
> *man in America, unless it were Thomas Jefferson, could*
> *have written.* (Frothingham, p. 68)

And Frothingham notes that by the time Everett left the editorship,
the journal sat on the tables of the most prestigious clubs, academies,
and libraries around the world (p. 67).

Finally, it must not be forgotten that Edward Everett did write two
books. First, during his exhausting tenure as pastor of the prestigious

Brattle Street Church, he found time to write a spirited, if not conse-
quential, five-hundred-page defense of Christianity entitled A Defense
of Christianity against the Work of George B. English (1814), about
which Bartlett writes:

> *The burden of this brief pastorate crushed Everett's nerves
> and forced a vacation. It did not interfere, however, with
> his ability to write a five-hundred-page book defending the
> authenticity of the New Testament against the attacks of
> George English, a renegade Harvard graduate. Successfully
> demonstrating that English had failed to understand the
> obscure Jewish writers he cited, Everett also proved that
> seventy-four pages of English's short, heretical volume were
> plagiarized. This scholarly, long-since-forgotten triumph for
> Unitarian orthodoxy was widely noticed and praised at the
> time and doubtless helped convince Everett that his destiny
> lay in the university rather than the church.* (p. 431)

His second book, Mount Vernon Papers, was a compilation of
the fifty-three articles he wrote between 1858 and 1859 for the New
York Ledger, a periodical owned by Robert Bonner. Thus, Everett
remained a man of letters throughout a career filled with sixteen-hour
days and a consuming private and public agenda.

EDWARD EVERETT: ORATOR AND STATESMAN

Paralleling his lifetime of public service is Edward Everett's career as
an orator. Whether performing the duties of a congressman, governor,
senator, foreign minister, secretary of state, or university president,
Edward Everett was first and foremost a public speaker. And he was
acclaimed in his day as America's greatest orator. Aside from his
sermons and his speeches in Congress, he delivered hundreds of
public lectures, eulogies, ceremonial addresses, and dedicatory orations, among which are a number of this nation's most important and
enduring texts as we shall see in further chapters.

Ralph Waldo Emerson referred to Edward Everett as *our Cicero*, the
illustrious statesman of the first century bce (before the common era)

who led the Roman republic during its finest years just prior to the rise of the Caesars. In the middle years of the nineteenth century, defined as they were by a robust revival of the classical texts of ancient Greece and Rome, no words of praise could have been more lavish. The study of rhetoric, once the heart of the curriculum in ancient Greece and Rome, was enjoying a renaissance in America as those millions of Americans new to Constitutional democracy looked to the public forum and the new class of professional orators to lead them through the nation's first decades of independence. And Cicero's works were at the very heart of that curriculum. We turn now to this newly revitalized study of rhetoric and oratory to see how it transformed scholars such as Edward Everett into the public voices of the *Golden Age of American Oratory.*

WORKS CITED

American Orators. Part 3, Vol. 8. New York: P. F.
    Collier and Son, 1900.

Bartlett, Irving. *Edward Everett Reconsidered,* New England
    Quarterly 69, 3 (September 1996): 429–60.

Brewer, David. Ed. The World's Best Orations. 11 vols. St. Louis
    and Chicago: Ferd
P. Kaiser, 1899.

DeNormandie, James, *Oration,* Centennial Anniversary of the Death
    of Edward Everett. Boston: Rockwell and Churchill, City
    Printers, 1895.

Edward Everett at Gettysburg. Boston: Massachusetts Historical
    Society.

Everett, Edward. Orations and Speeches on Various Occasions. 2
    Vols. Boston: Little, Brown, and Company, 1850.

Everett, Edward. Papers. Boston: Massachusetts Historical Society.
   Microfilm. 54 Reels.

Frothingham, Paul Revere. Edward Everett: Orator and Statesman.
   Boston: Houghton Mifflin Company, 1925.

Hamlin, Talbot. Greek Revival Architecture in America. New York:
   Dover
Publications, Inc., 1944.

Pryor, Elizabeth Brown. Robert E. Lee's 'Severest Struggle,
   American Heritage 58 (Winter 2008):18-33.

Reid, Ronald. Edward Everett: Unionist Orator. New York:
   Greenwood Press, 1990.

Varg, Paul. Edward Everett: The Intellectual in the Turmoil of
   Politics. London and Toronto: Associated University Presses
   1992.

Wills, Garry. Lincoln at Gettysburg: The Words That Remade
   America. New York: Simon and Schuster, 1992.

BOSTON LYCEUM.

PROGRAMM.

1834.

Oct. 23. Introductory Lecture, ... RUFUS CHOATE.

    30. Discussion. Does the multiplicity of societies at the present day, on the whole, impede individual action?

Nov. 6. Lecture. A Reform in Education, . . . E. M. P. WELLS.

    13. Lecture, ... EDWARD EVERETT.

    20. Lecture. Italy, ... H. T. TUCKERMAN.

    27. Lecture. Phrenology, ... N. JONES.

Dec. 4. Lecture. Self Education, ... B. B. THATCHER.

    11. Lecture. do. . . . . . B. B. THATCHER.

    18. Discussion. Does the welfare of our country, require any alteration of the Naturalization Laws?

    24. Lecture. Poetry of Mrs. Hemans, . . . B. B. THATCHER.

1835.

Jan. 1. Lecture. The progress of liberty in France, . AMASA WALKER.

    8. Lecture. Elocution, ... WM. H. SIMMONS.

    15. Lecture. Self Respect, ... G. S. HILLARD.

    22. Lecture, ... C. C. EMERSON.

    29. Discussion. Do moral or physical causes have the greatest influence in determining national character?

Feb. 5. Lecture, ... C. T. JACKSON.

    12. Lecture, ... NEHEMIAH ADAMS.

    19. Lecture, ... G. S. HILLARD.

    26. Lecture, ... J. A. BOLLES.

Mar. 5. Lecture, ... G. S. HILLARD.

    12. Discussion.

    19. Lecture, ... CHARLES SUMNER.

    26. Exhibition.

Other gentlemen, in the course of the season, may be invited to lecture before the Lyceum. Classes in Chemistry, Elocution, Geography and History, and the French language, will be formed under the direction of the Board of Managers.

Tickets at two dollars each, to admit a gentleman and ladies, may be obtained of Perkins, Marvin, & Co., T. A. Davis, Marsh, Capen, & Lyon, and James B. Dow.

Lyceum Program

2

The Golden Age of American oratory

Oratory is the masterful art. Poetry, painting, music, sculpture, architecture, please, thrill, inspire; but oratory rules. The orator dominates those who hear him, convinces their reason, controls their judgment, compels their action. For the time being he is master. Through the clearness of his logic, the keenness of his wit, the power of his appeal, or that magnetic something which is felt and yet cannot be defined, or through all together, he sways his audience as the storm bends the branches of the forest.... Who does not delight in oratory? Do we not all feel the magic of the power? And when occasionally we are permitted to listen to a great orator how completely we lose ourselves and yield in willing submission to the imperious and impetuous flow of his speech!

—*Supreme Court Justice David Brewer,* 1900

A CULTURE BUILT ON ORATORY

In the century from approximately 1820 to 1920, American oratory extended its reach beyond the nation's courtrooms, churches, and legislative halls to the public platform. By 1830, the typical American town would have had, at the very least, a debating club, a lecture series, and numerous ritualized holiday festival orations. In nineteenth-century America, no public event was complete without a speaker giving voice and meaning to the occasion. From these public forums and rituals, presided over by a phalanx of great orators who had been trained in classical rhetoric, sprang a *lively exchange of ideas* and, out of this exchange, the crafting of a uniquely American identity. Indeed, as rhetorician Angela Ray has commented, it was through the oratory of the nineteenth-century that America's *public selves and public cultures were constituted* (p. 7).

Halfway through the century, historian Edward Parker referred to this era as the *Golden Age of American Oratory* (Reid, 1990, p. 6), for in addition to the traditional judicial, legislative, and ecclesiastical forms, the era gave rise to the new genre of demonstrative oratory. One popular type of this innovation became known as the secular jeremiad, or lecture. The lecture, which historian Page Smith has defined as a *sermon that offers intimations of salvation without requiring the assumption of burdensome responsibilities* (4: 698), was a new medium of communication, unknown in the ancient world or even in modern Europe, through which the public could be informed, entertained, and inspired. Historian Donald Scott asserts that *The lecture system not only expressed a national culture; it was one of the central institutions within and by which the public had it existence* (Ray, p. 7).

Some lecturing forums were concerned with *the diffusion of practical knowledge,* an end to which Josiah Holbrook, the founder of the most popular public speaking circuit of the day, the Lyceum, specifically dedicated it in 1826. By 1844, between three thousand and four thousand town-sponsored lyceums (Bode, p. 12) were actively engaged in this uniquely American, democratic form of intellectual leveling, and it was through the Lyceum movement that many of the era's greatest figures began their careers as public speakers. Abraham Lincoln, for example, delivered his first public speech in 1838 to the Young Men's Lyceum in Springfield, Illinois.

In addition to lectures on science, agriculture, education, and practical living, audiences flocked to those on biography. Scott Casper refers to this popular theme as the medium through which people *peered into the lives of strangers* to learn about themselves. Casper notes that

> *Biographers, and critics, and readers alike believed that biography had power: the power to shape individuals' lives and character and to help define America's national character.* (p. 2)

The goal of shaping character was often guided by the idea of *greatness,* a theme that fascinated Americans. Lectures on how Napoleon or Oliver Cromwell or Benjamin Franklin achieved greatness were common, and from such examples, speakers derived qualities that ordinary Americans might emulate.

Other public addresses—like eulogies, holiday festival orations, speeches of dedication, or valedictory addresses—centered on ceremonial and commemorative events. Encomiums (speeches of praise) honored the Puritan or Pilgrim settlers, lauded the founders, or memorialized heroes and the significant battles they had waged to secure the nation's independence. The opening of a new school, the christening of a naval vessel, or even the establishment of a more humane prison—all required an oration to confer meaning upon them.

The typical festival oration was drenched in patriotism, and the orator's main duty was not to criticize but to praise. In the 1840s, however, radicals and reformers began to appropriate public forums to further social causes, especially the causes of abolition, prohibition, and women's rights. Fiery orators such as Wendell Phillips, William Lloyd Garrison, and Frederick Douglass provoked their audiences into shouting matches, occasional brawls, and even mob actions in and around the public forums. Female abolitionists and suffragists such as Sarah and Angelina Grimké, Abby Kelley Foster, and Lucy

Stone brought a woman's voice to the public stage as they raised the consciousness of the nation about human rights often while endangering their own lives. And temperance crusaders such as John B. Gough recounted conversion narratives that, while framed as entertainment, were designed to persuade the audience to take the pledge and cast out demon rum.

This was America in the mid-nineteenth century: a sometimes cacophonous, but more often inspiring, mélange of public voices making pronouncements on every imaginable topic on every public occasion. Historian of rhetoric Bower Aly captures the essence of the period when he notes that *Speechmaking went on in the daily exercise of life in situations and under circumstances that defy classification. And if no situation requiring speechmaking was at hand, then one was invented* (quoted in Clarke and Halloran, p. 14). The consistent purpose of the public forum, as rhetorical scholars Gregory Clarke and S. Michael Halloran note, *was to form and sustain a public consensus, intellectual and moral, as the basis of civic action* (p. 2).

By the 1850s, three decades into the Golden Age, professional orators were crisscrossing the country, projecting their vision of America's future and challenging their audiences to become a part of what they saw as a divinely inspired experiment in democracy. In towns and cities from coast to coast, week-long lecture programs attracted the new superstars of the lecture circuit, and by the onset of the Civil War, many had achieved wealth and celebrity for speeches that audiences loved to hear again and again.

The War Between the States closed down the national dialogue for four bloody years, but it would rise again in the 1870s, the Reconstruction era, in a new and modern venue, the Chautauqua. Along with its permanent site at Lake Chautauqua, New York, traveling Chautauquas, summer programs of usually a week's duration that were presented inside massive, brown canvas tents, were replete with music, entertainment, and, of course, oratory. Two Black Americans, Douglass and Booker T. Washington, were popular Chautauqua speakers who sought to reach across the racial divide to begin the nation's healing process. Female orators such as Frances Willard, Susan B. Anthony, Mary Livermore, and Elizabeth

Cady Stanton championed the cause of equal rights for women, and reformers such as Harvey Wiley, Judge Ben Lindsey, and Jane Addams discoursed about matters of public health and juvenile delinquency. The most popular orator of the day was, arguably, Russell Conwell, who offered an illustrious tribute to the Protestant work ethic known as *Acres of Diamonds*. With but that one speech in his repertoire, which he delivered some five thousand times, Conwell made enough money to found Temple University and the first free medical clinic in Philadelphia. Even famous writers such as Mark Twain and Edgar Allan Poe supplemented their authorial earnings with lucrative engagements on the Chautauqua circuit. While today the public airwaves produce the symbols and disseminate the ideas by which we live, in the nineteenth century, it was the orator, acting as both educator and entertainer, who defined and shaped the essential character of America.

EDWARD EVERETT AND THE GOLDEN AGE OF AMERICAN ORATORY

It was within this milieu of public culture making through oratory that Edward Everett came of age. He would rise to its heights, surpassing in both production and popularity all those who graced the ubiquitous public stages of the times. *His reputation extended to the country at large, and thousands came to hear him,* notes Paul Varg (p. 13). In 1858, on the second of his exhausting but exhilarating tours during which he delivered his legendary speech *The Character of Washington,* Everett was introduced to one audience of two thousand as *Orator, Patriot, Sage! Cicero of America, Laudator of Washington, Apostle of Charity, High Priest of the Union, and Friend of Mankind* (Ayres, pp. 2–3). In 1863, following the momentous battles at Gettysburg, David Wills and the other organizers of the solemn dedication ceremony knew immediately who they must secure to deliver the day's main oration: Edward Everett. And when he died two years later, it was said of him that *his name and his fame shall live forever* (Reid, 1956, p. 1). Looking back forty years later, David Brewer concluded, as did almost everyone, that the orator Edward Everett was, *elevated in his ideas, broad in his sympathies, unerring in his instinct of rectitude, and lacking almost nothing of the first rank as an orator and statesman* (p. 2091).

The lecture format was perfectly suited to Everett's talents and his temperament. To paraphrase Page Smith, the lecture is not designed for moments of crisis but for meditative times, when those in attendance may settle comfortably into their seats to be informed and entertained on the various truths of their age (p. 989). The lecture is the medium of the intellectual and the educator. It is designed for moderation and for a speaker whose message is constitutive of the values and virtues of the audience to whom the address is given. Everett, along with his student Ralph Waldo Emerson, raised this new genre to a form of high art, using it to spread his unique blend of *idealism* and *optimism* to millions of immigrants who were beginning to call themselves Americans.

In addition to his lectures, Everett was also responsible for bringing a timely and nostalgic *romanticism* into the public forum through his public eulogies and ceremonial addresses on festive or memorial occasions. At a time when the first generation of Americans, those from the founding period, were dying, and when their graves and the battlefields of the Revolutionary War were being set aside and consecrated, Edward Everett was the inevitable first choice to preside over the dedicatory event. Moreso than any other orator of his day, Everett mastered the rhetoric of *sentimentalism*. No one could praise a departing hero better than he.

With its signature mix of optimism, idealism, romanticism, and sentimentalism, Everett's oratory became unapologetically *patriotic*. He had faith in his country and in the Constitution upon which it was established. Today, the patriotism evident throughout his oratory might be characterized as conservative, and there were times when it would turn mawkish and blind him to larger causes. In his day, however, Everett gave his audiences what they wanted to hear and what he cherished most: love of country.

And because he was devoted to the Union forged in the Constitution, Everett's rhetoric was *conciliatory*. Like Emerson, he seldom engaged in polemics on the public platform. His brilliance was not in choosing sides but in seeing both. That same spirit of compromise that had drawn the states together into one nation, Everett believed, held the promise of preserving it. Even in the

Chautauqua Tent
Circa 1910

darkest moment of consecration during the Civil War, at Gettysburg
on November 19, 1863, when the nation's citizens turned to Edward
Everett to help them understand the carnage and sacrifice that had
become the thousands of gravestones before their eyes, he lifted their
spirits with the hope of reconciliation and a long period of peace.

During his forty-year career as a public speaker, Everett was the
figure primarily responsible for reviving oratory as *among the supreme
manifestations of art,* as Perry Miller would later put it (quoted by
Wills, p. 47). His lectures, festival orations, and commemorative
addresses are monuments to the classical epideictic, or ceremonial,
traditions of ancient Greece and Rome, when orators were expected to
rise above what Cicero once called *the daily noise* of the city. Everett
inspired and enchanted his audiences with words that often soared
above their own vocabularies, but they loved him for it. As the painter
uses his brush, so did Edward Everett use his voice. He worked in
words as the ancient Greek sculptor Phidias worked in marble.

Everett's style, marked by the erudition of his texts, the purity of his diction, the polished tones of his voice, and his stately manner of delivery, owed most, perhaps, to the fact that he was a master of language. While Emerson's signature was the aphorism or the *quotable quote,* Everett worked in figurative expressions such as metaphors, similes, allusions, and apostrophes. And where Emerson was epigrammatic, Everett was *periodic,* crafting complex sentences with antitheses and anaphoras that would build, clause by clause, to a climactic ending.[1] We can see (and hear) this periodic style clearly evident (with my emphasis) in the following string of sentences from Everett's August, 1826 eulogy to John Adams and Thomas Jefferson:

> *The contemporary and successive generations of men will disappear, and in the long lapse of ages, the races of America, like those of Greece and Rome, will pass away. The fabric of American freedom, like all things human, however firm and fair, may crumble into dust. But the cause in which these our fathers shone is immortal. They did that to which no age, no people of civilized men, can be indifferent. Their eulogy will be uttered in other languages, when those we speak, like us who speak them, shall be forgotten. And when the great account of humanity shall be closed, in the bright list of those who have best adorned and served it, shall be found the names of our Adams and our Jefferson.* (Everett, p. 149)

Finally, while Emerson's speeches were aimed at his audience's intuition; Everett struck at their imagination. As one observer put it,

> *He spoke as the ocean rolls in billows, in rhythmic measured sentences rising higher and higher, more and more translucent until they would break in the long sparkling surf and ripple along the sandy floor of the beach.* (Stebbins, p. 197)

---

1. See p. 86 for explanations of these terms.

Everett's flights of rhetorical fancy dominated an occasion, enveloping the audience in the pure aesthetic of beautiful words beautifully spoken. No one else of his day dared address an audience of ordinary citizens in Latin or ancient Greek or recite to them from Dante or Virgil, but Everett never hesitated. Although some of his orations would ascend to the status of literature, they were, as Everett noted in his Orations and Speeches, *written to be spoken* (I: viii); he intended not so much to awe his audience with his erudition as to celebrate with them the dignity of articulate speech. Yes, his oratory would have its mundane moments, its troughs, its grandiloquent excesses, and Everett himself would plead guilty to this charge in his collected works (1: vii–xii), but at their best, his public addresses set the standard for eloquence in an age when oratory was the Prince of the Arts (see Reid, 1990, p. 44; and Clarke and Halloran, introduction).

Starting as they did in the late 1820s and early 1830s, respectively, Everett and Emerson were the two earliest superstars of the lecture circuit, and they would continue to be so for the next forty years. They would provide the *uplift* Americans so reveled in and demanded by advancing the causes of patriotism, liberal individualism, popular democracy, and virtuous living. And they would do so not by posing as *merchants of perpetual sunshine* but by challenging their audiences to contemplate great ideas and consider lives of transcendent purpose. Between them, Everett and Emerson would define the word *American* and describe for the general public a soaring vision of the nation, one that would guide it to its first accomplishments in the secular worlds of the arts, letters, science, popular government, commerce, and education.

Everett, more so than Emerson, was the nation's high priest of optimism, its sage of sentimentality, and its voice of unabashed nationalism. Toward the end of his career, he became America's most eloquent eulogist. As may be seen from the chronology of his speeches presented in appendix A, Everett was equally at home dedicating a new high school, a new prison, or a national cemetery. And he was equally welcome and sought out in all parts of the country. During his four-decade-long career as a professional orator, Everett would speak on every topic from agriculture to youth, and he would speak to

everyone from schoolboys to presidents, from farmers to the Marquis
de Lafayette. In 1836, when Everett was already a sought-after orator
in New England but one who had not yet achieved national renown,
his former teacher John Quincy Adams wrote in his Journal that

> *Mr. E.E., now Governor of the Commonwealth, and Mrs.
> E., paid us a morning visit; and he gave me a volume of his
> orations and speeches recently published. They are among
> the best ever delivered in this country, and, I think, will
> stand the test of time.... Of the thousands and tens of thou-
> sands of these orations, which teem in every part of this
> country, there are, perhaps, not one hundred that will be
> remembered "Alteri seculo,"[2] and of them, at least one half
> have been, or will be, furnished by E.E. He has largely con-
> tributed to raise the standard of this class of compositions,
> and his eloquence has been the basement story of his political
> fortune—as yet, one of the most brilliant ever made in this
> Union. (Frothingham, p. 400)*

THE EDUCATION OF AN ORATOR IN THE NINETEENTH CENTURY
Everett's success as an orator sprang from his natural aptitude for
language, but that talent was cultivated by astute teachers who recognized it. Like so many educated men of his age, he was assiduously
trained in the newly revitalized discipline of rhetoric. American
universities established courses in the *science* of persuasive speaking
(rhetoric) and the practice of the *art* of oratory (eloquence) almost
as if on cue to help the new nation discover itself, provide it with its
voice, and become, as it has been throughout history, the *handmaiden
of democracy* (Murphy and Katula, p. 3).

The resurgence of training in rhetoric at the turn of the nineteenth
century was grounded in the principles of the ancient Greek and
Roman sophists, philosophers, and statesmen. Inspiration came in
waves from the ancient texts written during the first experiments in

---

2. "by future generations"

democracy and republican government between 500 bce and 200 ad. Everett and others of his generation drew inspiration from words such as these written by the Greek philosopher Isocrates in his essay *Nicocles*:

> *In most of our abilities we differ not at all from the animals; we are in fact behind many in swiftness and strength and other resources. But because there is born in us the power to persuade each other and to show ourselves whatever we wish, we not only have escaped from living as brutes, but also by coming together have founded cities and set up laws and invented arts, and speech has helped us attain practically all of the things we have devised.... By speech we refute the wicked and praise the good. By speech we educate the ignorant and inform the wise. We regard the ability to speak properly as the best sign of intelligence, and truthful, legal, and just speech is the reflection of a good and trustworthy soul.... If I must sum up on this subject, we shall find that nothing done with intelligence is done without speech, but speech is the marshal of all actions and of thoughts, and those most use it who have the greatest wisdom.*
> (Murphy and Katula, p. 56)

Writing in the fourth century bce, Isocrates believed that oratory should serve the cause of *panhellenism*, or what we would today call the common good. Isocrates spoke against the politics of pure expediency, arguing that the orator must emphasize honor and justice above all else—that these were the moral, and hence real, expedients of a democratic society (Kennedy, p. 198). Of Isocrates' school, which included the most influential citizens of the Greek city-states, Cicero commented, *As from the Trojan horse, none but real heroes proceeded* (Murphy and Katula, p. 51).

Isocrates had a lasting influence on the science of rhetoric, not only in his day and during the republican period of the Roman empire, but even into the revolutionary era and America's first decades of independence. His idea that the statesman is a man who studies philosophy and rhetoric and who speaks for the best interests of his country (over individual or sectional interests) would weigh heavily on that generation of American young men charged with institution- alizing the ancient ideals embedded in the Constitution. Edward Everett was among them.

Isocrates maintained that oratory was the consummate art, much more difficult to master than the others—mathematics, poetry, phi- losophy—and much more powerful in its application to real world problems. Cicero echoed Isocrates' belief, arguing not only that the orator must master all fields of knowledge, because oratory encom- passed them all, but that he must give them life through the power of expression. Cicero's beliefs about rhetoric and eloquence are no more clearly expressed than when he writes that

> *Oratory demands knowledge of many subjects, mastery of style, understanding of men's emotions, a charming, cul- tured wit, a memory filled with history, comprehension of civil law. In addition, oratory demands an understand- ing of delivery and a commanding memory. Since oratory demands so much we can understand why its ranks number so few.* (Murphy and Katula, p. 167)

Cicero's writings on rhetoric and oratory were an essential guide in nineteenth-century education in America, and the study of rhetoric soon emerged as the centerpiece of a young American's education, from the child's earliest learning experiences and through matriculation at an academy or college. Edward Everett was no exception. At the memorial service following his death, Everett's eulogist, the Reverend Elias Nason, recounts Everett's introduction to the study of the art of eloquence. It is so beautifully composed, albeit in the sometimes antiquarian style of the day, I could not improve upon it. At the risk of over-quoting, and with some minor editing of extraneous details, it is reprised here as it was presented on January 17, 1865, to the membership of the New England Historic-Genealogical Society on Bromfield Street, Boston, Massachusetts:

"Young Edward began his education at the village school on Meeting-house Hill, in his native town, under the charge of Miss Lucy, daughter of Noah Clapp, Esq. He was then three years old; and his first misfortune in life, he himself has said, was the loss of the 'blue paper cover from one corner' of his primer, which then constituted his whole library. He came afterwards, while in Dorchester, under the instruction of the Rev. J.B. Howe and Rev. W. Allen; and here commenced his oratorical career by the recitation, at a public exhibition, of the 'Little Roan Colt,' –

'Pray how should I, a little child,
In speaking make a figure? –'

written expressly for him by his affectionate pastor, who, in the expression 'little roan,' refers to the color of his curling hair.

Soon after the decease of his father, which produced a profound impression of sorrow upon the tender mind of Edward, the family removed to Boston, where at the age of nine (April, 1803), he commenced attending the public reading and writing school taught by Masters Little and Tileston, in North Bennet Street. Mr. Ezekiel Little, a graduate of Harvard College in 1784, was a popular instructor in his day, and with the aid of Mr. Caleb Bingham's two excellent class reading-books, the Columbian Orator and the American Preceptor, succeeded in teaching his pupils how to read with animation and propriety, and in inspiring them with a love of declamation. We may easily conceive how modestly, and yet how beautifully, the young orator would pronounce such pieces as –

'You'd scarce expect one of my age
To speak in public on the stage,'

which his clever kinsman, Mr. David Everett, had furnished for the former school-book; or with what winning grace he

would repeat such patriotic lines as Dr. Dwight's in the
latter's excellent work,--
> 'Columbia! Columbia! To glory arise, –
> The queen of the world and the child of the skies,' –

for, even in early boyhood, he possessed a boy's sweet, silvery
eloquence. His other teacher, John Tileston, was what might
be called a 'character.' He was an old man (having been
born in Braintree in 1738), who wore a large horse-hair wig,
and who wiped the ink from the pen on his little finger, and
then from his finger on the frosty locks just beneath his bushy
peruke. He was short and thick; and although his right
hand had been burned, and the chords of it drawn together,
his penmanship was quite respectable; and he taught the boy
– of whom he afterwards became so proud – that plain, even,
clear, characteristic handwriting which he retained even up
to that touching letter written to his daughter two days before
his death, in which he says alluding to his indisposition, 'I
have turned the corner. Ever your affectionate papa, E. E.'

As these early, fostering influences have such a direct bear-
ing on the stately tree that rises heavenward by them and
through them, you will pardon me, I feel assured, for quoting
a few lines from a speech in which Mr. Everett himself refers
to his teachers and his studies in the North Bennet-street
School: 'Master Little, in spite of his name, was a giant in
stature, — six feet four at least, — and somewhat wedded to
the past. He struggled earnestly against the change then tak-
ing place in the pronunciation of u, and insisted on our say-
ing monooment and natur. But I acquired under his tuition
what was thought, in those days, a very tolerable knowledge
of Lindley Murray's abridgment of English grammar; and,
at the end of the year, could parse almost any sentence in the
American Preceptor. Master Tileston was a writing-master
of the old school. He set the copies himself, and taught that
beautiful old Boston handwriting, which, if I do not mistake,

has, in the march of innovation, been changed very little for the better. Master Tileston was advanced in years, and had found a qualification for his calling as a writing-master in what might have seemed, at first, to threaten to be an obstruction. The fingers of his right hand had been contracted and stiffened in early life by a burn, but were fixed in just the position to hold a pen and a penknife, and nothing else. As they were also considerably indurated, they served as a convenient instrument of discipline. A copy badly written, or a clotted page, was sometimes visited with an infliction which would have done no discredit to the beak of a bald eagle.... I desire, however, to speak of him with gratitude; for he put me on the track of an acquisition which has been extremely useful to me in after-life, — that of a plain, legible hand. I remained at these schools about sixteen months, and had the good fortune, in 1804, to receive the Franklin medal in the English department.'

The future orator was fortunate in his instructors; for, on leaving the North Bennet-street School, he entered that of Mr. Ezekiel Webster, whose mental powers were equaled only by those of his brother Daniel, who for a brief period had the school in charge.

What secret aspirations for honorable fame were awakened, what hidden springs of thought were set in motion, what sacred fires were kindled in the grateful pupil's breast, by these two master-minds, we cannot tell; yet this we know, that a sympathy and affection were engendered here, the tranquil surface of whose strong current political rivalries could not ruffle, but which moved along broader and deeper to the unsounded ocean of eternal love; and of it the immortal jurist has thus touchingly remarked: 'We now and then,' writes he to Mr. Everett, under date of July 21, 1852, see stretching across the heavens a clear, blue, cerulean sky, without cloud or mist or haze; and such appears to me our acquaintance, from the time when I heard you for a week recite your lessons in the little schoolhouse in Short Street to the date hereof.'

The next year (1806), young Everett entered the Latin School, then on School Street, and under the care of the learned but eccentric William Biglow. This instructor was an ardent lover of the languages, had written one or two school-books, and possessed in a remarkable degree the ability of inspiring the minds of his pupils – and this is one of the highest qualifications of an educator – with a love of learning and philosophy.... His encouraging exhortation to his pupils used to be, —

'First learn to write, then to indict,
And then a line of Latin;
And so by chance you may advance
To wear a suit of satin.'

Under the tuition of Mr. Biglow, Everett read, as if by intuition, Caesar, Cicero's Orations, parts of Virgil, and the Greek Testament. The study of the languages was at that period extremely superficial. The analysis of sentences, the derivation of words, the philosophy of the subjunctive mode, the delicate shades of meaning expressed by the conjunctions, particles, and expletives, received but little or no attention; for the light of German philology had not as yet dawned upon this country: but Edward Everett received with great avidity such instruction as was then imparted, and made such progress in the classics as to secure again the Franklin medal for 1806; thus giving another earnest of a brilliant literary career.

At the age of thirteen, — that is, in the early part of 1807, -- he entered Phillips Exeter Academy, then under the judicious care of Dr. Benjamin Abbott, and there completed the studies

*preparatory to his admission to Harvard College in the
autumn of the same year. The school was then, as at present,
the Rugby of New England; and the 'gentlemanly Edward,'
as he was termed, here soon acquired the esteem of teachers and associates, together with the enviable reputation of
being a faithful, industrious, and brilliant scholar.... His
brother (the late Alexander Hill Everett) and Mr. Nathan
Hale were assistant teachers in the institution; and Edward
had his room with them at Mrs. Benjamin Conner's, on
the south side of Front Street, between the academy and the
river. Though a mere stripling, the ambitious schoolboy, on
his first entrance into the recitation-room, as if conscious of
his power, marched up, and took his place at the head of the
Latin class; nor did he fail to retain that enviable position
to the end. He is remembered as being then slender in form,
neat in dress, and polite and dignified in manner. His hair
was a fine auburn, or what the Latins might have termed
flavus; and his voice had a silvery sweetness, —*

'So soft, so clear,
The listener held his breath to hear.'

*He read his favorite Tully and Virgil with ease and fluency;
so that the Latin seemed as a new and living language on
his melodious tongue. His eye was quick as an electric flash
to discern a touch of grace or beauty in a classic writer;
and his critical acumen, his insight into the meaning, his
apprehension of the spirit of an ancient author excited
constant admiration in the mind of the instructor. In
declamation as in the class-recitations, young Everett stood
primus inter pares.*[3]

*The society of Exeter was at that period noted for its learning
and refinement, and doubtless shed a genial influence upon
the opening powers of the aspiring student. At the close of his*

---

3. *first among equals.*

academical career, during which he had won the good will of those who knew him, he pronounced the salutatory oration in Latin, which Dr. Abbott kept as a model of elegant Latinity for succeeding boys to imitate, and bequeathed to his able successor, Dr. Soule, as a rich legacy. It is written in Mr. Everett's well-known and beautiful style of penmanship imparted by the venerable John Tileston, and commences with a fine allusion to the brightness of the day and the dignity of the assembly. It is a remarkable specimen of composition in a dead language for a boy of only thirteen summers, and shows how well his taste and his ear had even then been trained. The delivery is said to have been as graceful as the language itself was elegant. The young orator received with reverent attention the instructions of Dr. Abbott, then in his prime: he sought for knowledge with such avidity as the bee seeks for nectar; and what he once secured he never lost. He seemed even then to have realized with Hesiod, that 'the gods have placed sweat in the pathway to excellence;' and he was willing to go through the one in order to attain the other.

Entering Harvard College in the autumn of 1807 as the youngest member of his class, he came immediately under the instruction of the accomplished Levi Frisbie, then tutor in Latin, who was himself a poet, and had the rare faculty of investing the driest principles of grammar with the golden glow of a brilliant imagination, and of enchanting the minds of his class with his elegant impromptu disquisition on the advantages and amenities of literature. John Quincy Adams also, to whose memory as a teacher Mr. Everett has paid an eloquent tribute, was then electrifying the college and the citizens of Cambridge with his lectures on rhetoric, which his future eulogist [Everett] heard with rapt attention and delight, and which doubtless exercised a potent influence in elevating his conceptions of the grand and beautiful, in chastening his imagination, and in perfecting his taste." (39–50)

From these early experiences, and from the influential teachers so vividly described by Nason, Edward Everett became a young man of refinement and taste with a keen sensitivity to language, especially the spoken word. By the age of thirteen, he was a master of English, Latin, and ancient Greek, had an intrinsic love of learning, and had discovered and polished his speaking voice through years of practice in declamation (reciting poems and speeches). Indeed, no young man in America was more ready by nature and training to internalize the instruction he received in college than Edward Everett, and there was no better teacher of rhetoric than the man who would become the sixth president of the United States, John Quincy Adams.

John Quincy Adams had been installed as the first Boylston Professor of Rhetoric and Oratory at Harvard University in June 1806. Serving in this position until 1809, he delivered one lecture per week until he resigned to become America's first minister to Russia. Before he left the university, his students asked that he allow his lectures to be published, an appeal to which he assented with some reservation. Fortunate it is for us that he did, however, for those thirty-six lectures comprise both a theoretical and historical account of how rhetoric and oratory were taught at distinguished institutions such as Harvard to those young gentlemen who, it was hoped, would lead the nation through its first generation of independence. Edward Everett was first among that cohort.

John Quincy Adams is the teacher we would all wish to have. He was brilliant and he loved what he was doing; he was demanding but devoted to his students; he was a patriot who loved his country. In his Inaugural Oration, delivered at his installation, Adams said this to his students:

> *Is there among you a youth whose bosom burns with the fires of honorable ambition; who aspires to immortalize his name by the extent and importance of his service to his country; whose visions of futurity glow with the hope of presiding in her councils, of directing her affairs, of appearing to future ages on the rolls of fame, as her ornament and pride? Let him catch from the relics of ancient oratory those unresisted*

> *powers, which mould the mind of man to the will of the*
> *speaker, and yield the guidance of a nation to the dominion*
> *of his voice* (1:30).

Inspirational words, indeed, and filled with the idealism and patriotism that would later define Everett's oratory. He would be one of those *youths* snared in the net of Adams's passion for reasoned discourse and his belief that

> *It is by the means of reason, clothed in speech, that the most*
> *precious blessings of social life are communicated from man*
> *to man, and that supplication, and praise are addressed to*
> *the Author of the universe* (1:14–15).

The thirteen-year-old Everett, then Harvard's youngest student, was a regular at Adams's morning lectures, and he practiced his declamations in the afternoon under Adams's tutelage. He was later taught by the second Boylston Professor of Rhetoric and Oratory, Joseph McKean, but Adams's influence is indelibly stamped into the oratory with which Everett would later inspire, educate, and delight the nation.

The study of oratory under John Quincy Adams was a journey through the classical writings of ancient Greece and Rome, especially those of Aristotle, Cicero, and Quintilian (all of whom were disciples of Isocrates), augmented with examples of memorable discourse from the ancients to the moderns, from Demosthenes to Edmund Burke. Of this pantheon of orators and theorists, Cicero was the greatest, *the friend of the soul,* Adams concluded, *whom we can never meet without a gleam of pleasure; from whom we can never part, but with reluctance* (1:115). Adams adopted the definition of rhetoric offered by Cicero's disciple, the Roman jurist Quintilian, that *rhetoric is the science of speaking well.*

Quintilian used the Latin phrase vir bonus dicendi peritus to describe the perfect orator: *the good man speaking well* (Murphy and Katula, pp. 201206). The good man speaking well was the citizen who took it as his public duty to speak for the good of the community, to advance the affairs of the empire, and to lead others by the force of his eloquence. Quintilian believed, as did the Roman historian Tacitus, that *Great eloquence, like fire, grows with its material, and becomes fiercer and brighter as it burns* (Murphy and Katula, p. 202). Following the exhortation of Tacitus, Adams predicted that should his students read widely, study logic, prepare their orations with great care and patience, and then engage in reasoned discourse, they too would lead their countrymen with distinction. *And who can doubt,* he emphasizes in Lecture 1,

> *but that in the sacred desk, or at the bar, the man who speaks well will enjoy a larger share of reputation, and be more useful to his fellow creatures, than the divine or the lawyer of equal learning and integrity, but unablest with the talent of oratory?* (p. 46).

Adams followed Cicero in dividing the study of rhetoric into its traditional five *canons*: the invention of ideas and arguments to bring reason and evidence to the topic; the organization of the speech to assure that the topic is covered thoroughly; style or the use of language to bring vivacity to one's ideas; memorization of the oration so that the focus will be on the audience; and delivery, both in gesture and voice, to give drama and excitement to the address. He covered each subject exactly as did the ancients, adding his own vivid examples from the entire literary corpus of Western civilization to urge his students forward in their pursuit of eloquence.

Adams then divided the speech into four general parts. The exordium was intended to establish good will, announce the theme of the address (statement of controversy), and make necessary digressions to adapt it to local concerns. The narration was intended to establish the context of the address by relating the story or recounting the history of the person or event under consideration. The partition and confirmation/refutation served the purpose of stating the subject of the address and then proving it through reasoned discourse while disproving the arguments of others. Finally, the peroration brought the entire oration to a sense of psychological closure through a tightly knit condensation of key ideas and an inspirational exhortation to the audience.

Adams then offered a catalog of rhetorical strategies, the *internal topics,* available to the orator when he composed his speech. These topoi are appropriate to any kind of speech, and they insure that the orator will have surveyed his topic comprehensively and located all pertinent arguments. Adams taught the following:

> *The internal topics are said to be sixteen; three of which, defi-*
> *nition, enumeration, and notation or etymology, embrace*
> *the whole subject. The others, without being equally compre-*
> *hensive, are derived from its various properties, incidents,*
> *and relations. From their names you will perceive the neces-*
> *sity of some further explanation to render them intelligible.*
> *They are as follows: genus, species, antecedents, consequents,*
> *adjuncts, conjugates, cause, effect, contraries, repugnances,*
> *similitude, dissimilitude, and comparison.* (1:209)

Everett's favorite topoi, as we will see demonstrated in his lectures, was *comparison,* and he used it repeatedly throughout his oratorical career, for it provided him with a device for clearly viewing America against the backdrop of other times and ages: ancient Greece, the Roman republic, Europe, etc.

Having now at his disposal a broad array of potential means for making arguments, Adams instructed his young orators that there were three modes of proof.[4] The first mode, *ethos,* arises from the character, good will, and erudition of the speaker. Everett and his fellow students would learn that the orator who would lead the nation must be a man of *enlarged and enlightened morality,* integrity, unim-peachable character, and temperance. Adams speaks with passion about the importance of ethos, and he finds it most essentially cap-tured in the phrase *an honest heart*:

> *It is unquestionably true, that in forming that ideal model*
> *of an all-accomplished orator, that perfect master of the art,*

---

4. The word *proof* as used by the Adams and the ancients may be thought of as *persuasion.*

> *which a fruitful imagination is able to conceive, the first*
> *quality, with which he should be endowed, is uprightness*
> *of heart.* (1:345)

The second mode of proof is *pathos.* The speaker must be passionate about his topic, and he must communicate that passion through his voice, gestures, and word choice, especially imagery that gives substance to abstract ideas and feelings. *Fluency of speech, strength of lungs, and boldness of heart* are the indispensable qualities of a distinguished orator, taught Adams. The speaker must also convey confidence, modesty, and benevolence. When the orator communicates those attributes to his audience, Adams declared, the audience returns them to him. Most important to an understanding of Everett's oratory is Adams's admonition to control the darker passions.

> *The Christian morality has commanded us to suppress the*
> *angry and turbulent passions in ourselves, and forbids us*
> *to stimulate them in others.... Addresses to the malevolent*
> *passions are not necessary for the highest efforts of eloquence.*
> (1:373)

None of the emotional fervor in a speech may be contrived; authenticity is the soul of great oratory, Adams concluded, and passion only proceeds from one's belief in what one is saying.

The essence of great oratory, however, lies in the third and most important mode of proof, *logos,* or reason. The orator must be knowledgeable, not only about the liberal arts but about practical matters as well. But because *art is long and life is short,* Adams noted, the orator cannot know everything. Thus, he must study methodically, reflecting carefully on what he reads and hears and allowing new ideas to change his way of thinking. *Let the streams of knowledge never stagnate upon your souls,* Adams admonished his young charges, because *indolence is like the sword of a hero in the hand of a coward* (1:362).

These three modes of proof—ethos, pathos, and logos—Adams emphasized, must work together to produce an oration that is credible, compelling, and convincing. Thus did the great teacher offer his students a complete *grammar* of rhetoric, the templates upon which they might come to build great orations. Adams then went on to demonstrate that process with a series of lectures so brilliant that they attracted not only his students but large crowds from the Cambridge and Boston communities.

In what remains, perhaps, his most original lesson, Lecture 10: Demonstrative Oratory, Adams planted the seeds that would soon blossom into that powerful American innovation, the lecture. In the lesson, Adams divided public addresses into four genres: deliberative speeches to be given in legislative bodies such as Congress; judicial arguments to be given at the bar; religious sermons to be delivered from the pulpit; and demonstrative orations (the kind for which Everett would become famous) to be presented on civic occasions. Since the lecture had yet to be developed as an independent form, Adams could provide little wisdom for those students, like Everett, who would later perfect this medium. He did, however, make the central point that

> *Whenever you shall have the occasion to speak in public, the first object, to which your attention will be required, can be no other, than to ascertain precisely the state of the controversy, or in other words the subject of your discourse. The next will be to collect from the whole stock of your ideas, those which may be most subservient to the design, for which you are to speak.* (1:230)

The speaker should be clear and direct in this regard: every speech has a central purpose that has called it into existence. This central purpose, the state of the controversy, must be firmly instilled in the minds of the audience so that they can meditate on the ideas the orator goes on to present in support of it. Clear, precise statements of purpose, as we will see, would become a central feature of an Everett oration.

Adams had a great deal to say about the other form of demonstrative oratory, the panegyric. A panegyric is a public speech delivered for the purpose of dispensing praise or blame. It is the appropriate mode of discourse for a eulogy or a memorial address about a distinguished personage; at public anniversary memorials such as the Fourth of July; or at public ceremonies dedicating a monument, battlefield, or cemetery. Panegyrics are important to a society for two reasons. First, borrowing from Cicero, Adams observed that *The approbation, the applause of their fellow men, are among the most precious rewards, which prompt the most exalted spirits to deathless achievements* (1:233).

Second, panegyric is the perfect medium through which to review and reinvigorate for the audience those virtues to which the society is dedicated. In order to accomplish these two objectives, the speaker must survey and address three topics. Adams adopts those listed in the ancient text on rhetoric, the ad herennium:[5] qualities of mind or character (virtues), bodily accomplishments (health, beauty, strength, long life, etc.), and external circumstances (status of family, wealth, education, etc.). Although the latter two topics are important, the focus must be on the first, the qualities of the person's mind or character, since these alone may be passed on as exempla for future generations. And in this matter the orator takes on his most important and difficult role: he becomes more than a biographer; he becomes an arbiter.

In a panegyric, Adams notes, the orator is charged with determining whether a person lived virtuously or not and to what degree. In order to do justice to his subject, therefore, the orator must understand the nature of each virtue, its antithesis, and where within those boundaries his subject falls. He must then judge and express that condition in words. To help his young orators make such critical judgments, Adams turned to Aristotle's treatise Nichomachean Ethics.

In Nichomachean Ethics, Aristotle develops his theory of virtue, sometimes known as the *theory of the mean,* or the Golden Mean. The philosophy of the Golden Mean begins with the assertion that a virtuous life is one defined by balance and proportion (harmony); the virtuous life, in other words, is conducted in a manner that is neither

---

5. In Adams' day, the *ad herennium* was thought to have been a treatise written by Cicero. It has since been assigned to an "unknown" author or to [Cicero]. See Caplan, Harry, [Cicero] *ad herennium, Loeb Classical Library, 1957, Introduction.*

excessive nor deficient but appropriate to the situation. As Aristotle says, *Being angry is easy, but being angry at the right time, for the right reason, and in the right way, that is very difficult.* The challenge of living virtuously presents itself most importantly in the balance one achieves between personal interests and the larger good of the community. The result of living according to the mean is worth the effort as it leads to *happiness* (eudaimonia), the telos or appropriate end all humans and all societies seek. *Happiness* itself is the mean point between the utopian *Good* (kalon) pursued by the Socratics and instant gratification or *Pleasure* (hedone), the goal attributed to the Sophists, those ancient teachers of rhetoric or the art of persuasion. To judge whether a person has achieved the mean, lived virtuously, and died happily, Aristotle provides nine virtues that serve as the scales upon which a person's life may be weighed: justice, fortitude, temperance, magnificence, magnanimity, liberality, meekness, prudence, and wisdom. He who achieves the proper balance between the pursuit of his own ends and the pursuit of society's larger purposes through the appropriate exercise of these virtues is a person of high character, and is to be congratulated for having demonstrated civitas or civic virtue.

In assaying the virtues and measuring his subject by them, the orator must decide whether a particular act was *rash, courageous,* or *cowardly,* the excessive, the mean, and the deficient forms of the virtue *temperance.* He must decide whether the deceased lived *prudishly, prudently,* or *self-indulgently*; *shamelessly, modestly,* or *reclusively*; and so on. Having made these calculations, the eulogist must sum up his subject's life in carefully chosen words, finding in it whatever lessons it may have to offer future generations.

But although a panegyric may assign both praise and blame, Adams emphasizes that for public eulogies (that form of panegyric known as *encomium*), *It has not, I believe, been the custom of any age or nation thus to administer censure* (1:237). While all demonstrative rhetoric has, like the bee, the capacity both for making honey and stinging, Adams asserts that for encomia, *Invective is not one of the pleasing functions of oratory* (I: 238). Thus, while the orator should never deviate from the truth, he may impose a *veil of silence* on the occasion, subordinating the individual's deficiencies and/or excesses (the vices) while celebrating his virtues so that they might serve the community's larger good. Here is the critical passage from Lecture 10 that would animate Everett's rhetoric:

> *The rules for the composition of panegyric are neither numerous nor complicated. The first is a sacred and undeviating regard for truth. But the duties, which truth prescribes, are variously modified under various relations. A mere biographer is bound to divest himself of all partialities; to notice the errors and failings, as well as the virtues and achievements of his hero. The obligation of the panegyrist is less rigorous. His purpose is not history but encomium. He is bound to tell the truth. Errors, vices, follies, must not be disguised nor justified; but they may be covered with a veil of silence; and if more than counterbalanced by transcendent merits, they may even be extenuated; a proceeding perfectly consistent with the pure morality of that religion, which teaches, that "charity" covereth a multitude of sin.* (1:247)

For Adams, the orator's legitimate, overarching goals dictate the way in which a subject's life should be approached. To advance the common good, he encourages the eulogist to apply the standard he calls *moral approximation.* Moral approximation involves deciding, for instance, whether an act the orator might normally regard as excessive or deficient might charitably be nudged slightly into its *mean* form. Or, perhaps an excessive or deficient behavior might even be subordinated, or *veiled,* in deference to some larger lesson the orator seeks to impart. The audience expects the orator to make such judgments; he is a man of integrity, no doubt, and he knows best what is appropriate. Adams notes,

> *To deny the speaker of panegyric the use of the faculty, which
> darkens or illumines the canvass of his portraits, would be a
> restriction too severe. He may present the object in the aspect
> best suited to his purpose, without deviating from the truth.*
> (1:248)

These two rhetorical strategies, the *veil of silence* and the
moral approximation, have a long history in oratory. They are
most notably manifest in the archetypal excerpt from the Funeral
Oration delivered by the ancient Athenian general Pericles at the
state funeral for the Athenian dead following the first year of the
Peloponnesian War in 430 bce:

> *To me it seems that the consummation which has overtaken
> these men shows us the meaning of manliness in its first
> revelation and in its final proof. Some of them, no doubt,
> had their faults; but what we ought to remember first is their
> gallant conduct against the enemy in defense of their native
> land. They have blotted out evil with good and done more
> service to the commonwealth than they ever did harm in
> their private lives. No one of these men weakened because he
> wanted to go on enjoying his wealth; no one put off the awful
> day in the hope that he might live to escape his poverty and
> grow rich. More to be desired than such things, they chose to
> check the enemy's pride. This, to them, was a risk most glori-
> ous, and they accepted it, willing to strike down the enemy
> and relinquish everything else. As for success or failure, they
> left that in the doubtful hands of Hope, and when the reality
> of battle was before their eyes, they thought it more honor-
> able to stand their ground and suffer death than to give in
> and save their lives. So they fled from the reproaches of men,
> abiding with life and limb the brunt of battle; and, in a
> small moment of time, the climax of their lives, a culmina-
> tion of glory, not of fear, were swept away from us.* (Murphy
> and Katula, p. 244)

Pericles chooses to honor, not censure, the dead. They were ordinary men who, he admits, *no doubt had their faults* but who also, at a critical moment in time, rose above their own fears to perform an extraordinary deed: give their lives for their country. On balance, then, these men are heroes, allowing Pericles to conclude that, *they have blotted out evil with good and done more service to the commonwealth than they ever did harm in their private lives.* At this oratorical occasion, when the purpose is to strengthen the nation's commitment to war as its spirits ebb, the focus must be on the fact that these soldiers loved their country enough to die for it. They did the right thing at the right time and, therefore, more than balanced their follies and vices with valor. Pericles is thus justified in taking the rhetorical turns of *moral approximation* and the *veil of silence.*

Everett would appropriate these rhetorical strategies throughout his career, especially in his festival orations and public eulogies. At the Charlestown Lyceum in 1830, for example, while speaking on the anniversary of the Puritans' arrival in Massachusetts, Everett made the following observation:

> *Men who have been connected with the establishment of great institutions ought to be judged by the general result of their work. We judge of St. Peters by the grandeur of the elevation and the majesty of the dome, not by the flaws in the stone of which the walls are built. The fathers of New England, a company of private gentlemen, of moderate fortunes, bred up under an established church and an arbitrary and hereditary civil government, came over the Atlantic two hundred years ago. They were imperfect, they had faults, committed errors. But they laid the foundations of the state of things which we enjoy—of political and religious freedom; of public and private prosperity; of a great, thriving, well-organized republic. What more could they have done? What more could any men do?* (Orations and Speeches, 1:235–36)

Following Adams's rule that *The eloquence of sentiment speaks in round numbers, and never concerns itself about fractional parts,*

Everett applies a *veil* to achieve the sentiment appropriate to the
occasion. Because he is not the Puritans' biographer or historian,
he may forego the small details of their *imperfections, faults,* and
errors (slaughtering the Pequot Indians, for example, or exiling Anne
Hutchinson for daring to question the authority of the ministers) to
assess the greater good they bequeathed: the virtues of freedom, prosperity, and stability. The comparison to St. Peter's Basilica supports
the rule: even this greatest of all monuments to Christ has its flaws,
but because we are not examining it as architects or engineers, its
defects are irrelevant to the real *state of the controversy*: worship and
devotion. Everett applies the orator's right to discretion, not deception (after all, he does acknowledge that the Puritans had made mis-
takes), to assure that his audience is in the proper frame of mind to be
moved and inspired.

It is through the *veil of silence* he applies and the *moral approximations* he makes that Everett's rhetoric takes on the characteristics of
idealism, sentimentality, romanticism, and patriotism. He learned
these techniques well, adopted them purposefully, and deemed his
choices ethical and proper for his audiences and his time. He tells us
why in this revealing passage in the preface to the first volume of his
Orations and Speeches:

> *It has also been objected to the manner in which some topics
> in American history are treated in these addresses, that it
> runs into overstrained sentiment. I am aware that there is
> danger of falling into this fault in orations for the fourth of
> July and other great popular festivals. But it ought not to
> be forgotten that a somewhat peculiar state of things existed
> among us twenty or thirty years ago, calculated to give the
> character in question to the figurative literature of the day.
> The great rapidity with which the United States had grown
> up since the declaration of independence, had given that
> kind of importance to recent events,—that hold upon the
> imagination,—which in a slower march of things, can usu-
> ally be the result of nothing but a lapse of centuries. There*

*were still lingering among us distinguished leaders of the
revolutionary struggle. Our heroic age was historical, was
prolonged even into the present time; and the present and the
historical consequently acquired something of the interest of
the heroic past. Amidst all the hard realities of the present
day, we beheld some of the bold barons of our Runnymede
face to face. This tended to lift events from the level of dry
matter of fact into the region of sentiment. Other circumstances—some of them incidents of this state of things—
exerted a powerful influence in the same direction.... They
produce, if I mistake not, in the community at large, a feeling of comprehensive patriotism, which I fear has, in a con-
siderable degree, passed away. While it lasted, it prompted
a strain of sentiment which does not now, as it seems to me,
find a cordial response from the people of any part of the
country. Awakened from the pleasing visions of former years
by the fierce recriminations and dark forebodings of the present day, I experience the feelings of the ancient dreamer when
cured of his harmless delusions:*

> _____*me occidistis, amici,*
> *Non servastis, ait, cui sic extorta voluptas,*
> *Et demtus per vim mentis gratissimus error."*
> (pp. xxi)[6]

In addition to Adams's classroom teachings on demonstrative oratory, Everett was influenced in both his public lectures and his festival
orations by his mentor's instructions on that critical canon of rhetoric, style, or the aesthetics of expression, to which Adams devoted
Lectures 25–34. From these lessons, Everett learned the meaning of
eloquence.

Eloquence, Adams taught, consists of elegance, composition, and
dignity. Eloquence is about words: their choice, their arrangement,
and their decoration. The first requirement of being eloquent is to use

---

6. You have deprived me, friends, in robbing me of such pleasure
and in depriving me, against my consent, of so delicious a Deception.

pure English; the second requirement is to speak in a dignified manner while making one's meaning clear to the audience.

With regard to the selection of one's words, Adams urged a new approach. Although the pure form of Greek or Latin was recommended for public speaking in ancient times, that standard when applied to English might well hem in the fullness of the orator's range. And so Adams suggested that the speaker, while taking care to be neither indelicate nor affected, should be free to choose those words he thought would most effectively and efficiently accomplish his ends.

> *The speaker in popular assemblies must often relax the muscles of his grammatical prudery, and liberally lacker [lacquer] his discourse with phraseology familiar to his audience, though restricted within a narrow channel of circulation.... New ideas may claim of right the vehicle of new words. Obsolete expressions may without offence be roused from a slumber, which has been mistaken for death. Naturalization may be made easy to foreign terms, upon the fair condition of useful service; and the only sentence of eternal banishment from his lips, to which a speaker should doom any word significant of thought, is that which moral purity requires.*
>
> *Immodest words admit of no defence,*
> *For want of decency is want of sense.*
> (2:159)

By *dignity*, Adams meant that words must adorn a speech and raise it above the conversational. The orator should use an abundance of figurative expressions such as metaphor,[7] metonymy,[8] apostrophe,[9]

---

7. Transfering the meaning of one word to another.
8. The use of a word closely associated with the object meant.
9. Addressing an inanimate object such as a bust or painting as though it were alive.

personification,[10] synecdoche,[11] antithesis,[12] epanaphora,[13] allusion,[14] hyperbole,[15] and other tropes and schemes to incite his listener's imagination and to elevate the oration beyond the vernacular speech of the parlor or saloon. Finally, as noted earlier, (p. 57) sentences should be written to be heard rather than read, composed, that is, in the *periodic* style as Cicero himself was famous for doing. Adams concluded,

> *Obtain, then, a command over the language, in which you are to speak, as extensive as possible. When discoursing in public, let your choice of words be neither tainted with indelicacy, nor tarnished with affectation. Let your word bear the express image of your thought, and transmit it complete to your hearer's mind. You need then give yourself very little concern to inquire for the parish register of its nativity. Whether new or old, whether of Saxon or of Grecian parentage, it will perform its duties to your satisfaction, without at all impairing your reputation for purity of speech.* (2:159)

Adams's words had their desired effect on his star pupil. In addition, Everett immersed himself in the great texts of Western civilization, texts rich in rhetorical figures—figures he would imitate and allude to. His language was pure in Adams's sense of that term. Everett did not forego a Latinate expression when he thought it the perfect vehicle for his design. His words were chosen for the occasion and for the audience, and the figurative expression—the vivid metaphor or stately antithesis—was regularly called forth to capture the imagination and establish a resemblance between his thought and some other in order to illuminate it and color it to his intention.

---

10. Making a mute form animate; giving to an object the qualities of a person.

11. Defining the whole from some part of it.

12. Opposing thoughts contrasted in connecting clauses.

13. Using similar word forms to begin successive clauses.

14. An indirect reference through the use of a passage to some historical event or person.

15. An exaggeration for some intended effect.

Everett's mastery of style became legendary and was frequently heralded in the popular press. Of the moment during his 1833 Bunker Hill oration when Everett welcomed President Andrew Jackson to Boston, a reporter commented, *It was done in a strain of eloquence scarcely ever superseded on earth* (Reid, 1956, p. 277). That same year, following his Fourth of July oration, the Independent Chronicle and Boston Patriot called it *a splendid exhibition of genius, taste, and learning—glowing with exalted patriotism* (Reid, 1956, p. 277). Even Emerson would write in 1850 that a stump orator (not a pejorative term in the nineteenth century) of Everett's talent came *only once in an age* (Reid, 1956, p. 278).

Everett achieved this level of aesthetic excellence through painstaking composition. Writing and then rewriting each sentence until he was completely satisfied, he sprinkled them with allusions drawn from the great texts of Western civilization—some in Latin, some in Greek, some in English—to give the address elevation as well as ornateness. Yes, there were at times more of the *flowers of rhetoric* than the occasion demanded; Everett admitted as much in the preface to his Orations and Speeches:

> *When I was at college, the English authors most read and admired, at least by me, and I believe generally by my contemporaries, were Johnson, Gibbons, and Burke. I yielded myself with boyish enthusiasm to their irresistible fascination. But the stately antithesis, the unvarying magnificence, and the boundless wealth of diction of these great masters, amply sustained in them by their learning, their power of thought, and weight of authority, are too apt, on the part of youthful imitators, to degenerate into ambitious wordiness.* (1:viiviii)

Nevertheless, Everett's excesses were for the most part excused by his audiences. Even his critics, who, like Jared Sparks, more than once accused Everett of engaging in rhetoric that was *much more flowing and beautiful than the logic is convincing* (Reid, 1956, 276), did not attribute his lofty powers of linguistic elegance to arrogance but to genius, even if at times genius overwrought.

Like few other orators of his day or since, Everett knew the value of high rhetorical flourish, and when the occasion called for it, he could turn a phrase like no other orator of his time, save perhaps Lincoln. Here he is eulogizing the Marquis de Lafayette at Boston's Faneuil Hall in 1834:

> *You have now assembled within these celebrated walls, to perform the last duties of respect and love, on the birthday of your benefactor. The spirit of the departed is in high communion with the spirit of the place—the temple worthy of the new name which we now behold inscribed on its walls. Listen, Americans, to the lesson which seems borne to us on the very air we breathe, while we perform these dutiful rites! Ye winds, that wafted the Pilgrims to the land of promise, fan, in their children's hearts, the love of freedom! Blood, which our fathers shed, cry from the ground! Echoing arches of this renowned hall, whisper back the voices of other days! Glorious Washington, break the silence of that votive canvas! Speak, speak marble lips; teach us the love of liberty protected by law!* (Orations and Speeches, 1:524)

Everett's purity and grace are clearly on display in this passage as he animates the scene and lifts his audience above their own poor power of expression to praise the legendary hero Lafayette; he creates in them the mood necessary to be inspired by the moment, and he provides for them the words to say what they would have said themselves but could not. Notice how the sentences build one upon the other until they crescendo in his final appeal to remember Lafayette by remembering the cause for which he fought. This is the rolling, billowing, periodic style Everett's admirers loved. Notice the use of figurative expressions: the apostrophe to *Glorious Washington* breathes life into the portrait of the Father of His Country; the *communion* and *temple* metaphors drape Faneuil Hall with religious imagery; the personification of the *wind, blood,* the *echoing arches* bring energy into the room. These are devices to which the orator has clearly devoted much thought. They give the speech eloquence born of a dignity befitting the event itself. Adams must have been proud. Isocrates would have been proud.

And more so than any other speaker of his time, or even ours, Everett was the master of Cicero's admonition to alter styles within the same speech. Everett's orations were designed to control the mood of the audience, raising them up and then taking them down, from silence into cheers, from laughter to tears, from poetry to conversation, all through the artfulness of his words and voice. Testimony to Everett's eloquence, the power of which Justice Brewer references in the epigram that begins this chapter, runs throughout the newspaper accounts of and personal testimony to Everett's oratory. Here, for instance, is Rufus P. Stebbins writing in the Cornell Era magazine about the eulogy to Lafayette quoted above.

> *My eyes were riveted on him during all the preliminary exercises. He rose at last to speak. He laid his manuscript on a small table at his left hand, on which stood a tumbler and a pitcher of water. There was grace in the manner in which he laid down his manuscript. There was music in the first words he uttered, so distinctly were they enunciated.* (p. 196)

Stebbins goes on to describe the majestic eloquence with which Everett praised the departed hero. At one point, when Everett compared Lafayette to Napoleon in a complex periodic sentence, Stebbins recollects that,

> *At this point, I remember well how intense was the feeling of the audience; and Mr. Everett, gaining inspiration by the warm sympathy which was expressed by a silence growing more and more breathless, almost to painfulness, rising to the loftiness of his theme, continued, with increasing enthusiasm...: "And if there is a man in this assembly that would not rather have been Lafayette to refuse than Napoleon to bestow his wretched gewgaws; that would not rather have been Lafayette in retirement and obscurity than Napoleon*

*with an emperor to hold his stirrup; if there is a man who
would not have preferred the honest poverty of LaGrange
to the bloody tinsel of St. Cloud; that would not rather have
shared the peaceful fireside of the friend Washington than
have spurred his triumphant courser over the crushed and
blackened heaps of the slain, through the fire and carnage
of Marengo and Austerlitz, that man has not an American
heart in his bosom...." "He ought," cried the orator in
tones which shook the pillars of the vast hall as well as the
hearts of that vast audience, and which ring in my ears as
I write, "he ought, with all his garters, ribbons, and stars
upon him, to be bolted down with a golden chain to the blaz-
ing pavement of a palace court-yard, that when his lord
and master goes out to the hunt of beasts or of men he may
be there, the slave, to crouch down and let his majesty vault
from his shoulders to his saddle." At the last word the audience, which had been in a perfect tremor of excitement for
the last two minutes, burst into a perfect tumult of applause.
Handkerchiefs waved, hands clapped, hurrahs were uttered,
shouts went up, epauletted veterans on the platform struck
hands, and I think there were one or two bugle notes or
something from the band. Mr. Everett drew a long breath,
turned a little water from the pitcher into the tumbler, just
wet his mouth for the first time, and turning to the audience proceeded in a simple, conversational manner with his
address. It was like a change from the blackness, torrents,
the thunder peals, the lightning glare of a dog-day shower, to
the sweet fragrance and quiet beauty which comes on when
the tempest is overpast.* (p. 198)

Adams had emphasized the singular importance of memory in the
orator's bag of tricks. He must have it, Adams insisted, *not only in
subjection, but at all times ready and available to his service* (2:359).
One's memory was strengthened mostly by knowing one's subject
and sticking to the truth of it; *the discipline of persevering application,
exercise, and method,* (2:361) along with using certain contrivances

and mnemonic devices as an aid during the address, were also recommended. The orator should write the speech in composition form first and then commit it to memory simply by repeating it over and over again. The habit of learning by heart, Adams preached, requires the most diligent concentration, but he who would master his memory would enjoy the greatest rewards from his appreciative audiences. Adams quoted Quintilian on this point:

> *But if any man asks me what is the greatest, nay the only art of memory, my answer is, exercise; labor; much learning by heart; much meditation; and if possible, daily repeated; this is worth all the rest. Nothing thrives so much upon industry; nothing perishes so much upon neglect. Let then the practice be taught and made frequent in childhood; and whoever, at any period of life, would cultivate his memory, must submit to the disgust of going over and over what he has written, and already many times read.* (2:366)

Anything less, Quintilian argued, results in a stumbling, hobbling, hesitating mode of speech.

In a letter to a Mr. Thomas Allibone, Everett described his methods of composition, preparation, and delivery:

> *With respect to speaking memoriter, I write out all my elaborate passages beforehand, some passages two or three times over. These imprint themselves on my memory by writing them. For the body of the discourse, I find a little study sufficient, and the written text is not accurately followed except in a few passages.* (Frothingham, p. 392)

With the gift of his prodigious memory, Everett was thus spared the *disgust* about which Quintilian speaks. Everett rarely delivered a speech exactly as he had written it; rather, he was a master of the fine art of *spontaneity*. At a commencement dinner, for example, his address was interrupted with a sudden flash of lightning and a peal of thunder. Everett instantly departed from his text to quote a line from

the Roman poet Virgil in his Georgics IV, describing the thunder-
bolts of Jove beneath Mount Etna - and this in Latin: ac veluti, lentis,
Cyclopes fulmonia massis cum properant (Frothingham, p. 393).
Today, we refer to this practice as the art of *scripting and rescripting*, a
skill seen in only the most polished and gifted orators. Frothingham
provides a wonderful example of it from Everett's oratory:

> *A remarkable instance of this [his extraordinary memory]*
> *was when he gave one of his Phi Beta Kappa orations at*
> *Cambridge—a task which he accepted at short notice....*
> *Longfellow was the poet of the day, and his part on the pro-*
> *gram preceded the oration. What was the poet's surprise,*
> *after reading his verses, to hear Everett, a few minutes later,*
> *repeat with exquisite cadence and expression several of the*
> *lines of the unprinted poem which had impressed him, and*
> *which he memorized as they fell from Longfellow's lips—in-*
> *troduced, too, into the oration as though they belonged there,*
> *and had been carefully prepared beforehand.* (p. 392)

Needless to say, the audience was dazzled by this mental feat.

The art of delivery, which, as the evidence above amply dem-
onstrates, Everett had clearly mastered in the course of his career,
was the subject of John Quincy Adams's final lecture as Boylston
Professor. Returning to the rules laid down by Quintilian in the first
century ad, Adams divided the art of delivery into action and voice.
Action was the use of the body to gesture; voice was the articula-
tion of sounds to *electrify the sentiment* (2:377). Speak slowly and
loudly enough for all to hear, Adams advised, and use the magic of
the human voice to its fullest potential (2:381). Because the public
lecturer or festival orator is generally confined in his movements by
a lectern, Adams concentrated his comments on such physical attributes as posture, facial expression, and gesture:

> *The head should be kept in an erect position; steady, but*
> *not immoveable; avoiding on one hand the stiffness of a*
> *statue, and on the other the perpetual nodding vibrations of*

a Chinese image. The countenance should be firm, without any appearance of presumption or of bashfulness; and composed with equal exemption from all affectation of harshness or of levity. The eyes should not be fixed to any one spot, but move round to every part of the audience particularly addressed.... The eyebrows and shoulders should seldom or ever be marked by any perceptible motion.... The movements of the arm should commence from the elbow rather than from the shoulder. They should generally be from left to right; and very seldom from right to left. In extending the arm, the fingers should also be extended; and the left hand or arm should seldom or never attempt any motion by itself. Finally, let it be remembered that the movements of the hands should generally accompany the tones of the voice for the expression of passion but very rarely for the imitation of action.
(pp. 388–89)

And, of course, the speaker must never be a mime or an actor but at all times, and in all movements, himself.

To his manner of delivery, Everett brought an elocutionary stateliness. It is a rare mastery of eloquence that allows one to rise above the conversational, above the vernacular, not only in language but in tone and gesture; to hold the last syllable of a word just an instant longer than usual; to raise the right arm above the shoulder and sweep one's hand slowly from left to right. These are difficult maneuvers, and most speakers cannot perform them without noticeable artificiality, even inauthenticity. But Everett could strike a pose without seeming to: with him the head raised, the eyes gazing above the assemblage toward the heavens, the jaw locked in affirmation—all looked natural and seemed to say *listen, this is important.* The pregnant pause, the hand lifted slowly above the shoulder or tucked in the lapel—all seemed to signal to the audience *listen, this should be remembered.* Edwin Whipple wrote that Everett's voice was *melodious,* and James Spear Loring described Everett as having,

> *an exquisite voice, round, swelling, full of melody, particu-*
> *larly emotional; naturally grave, and with a touch almost*
> *of melancholy in some of its cadences, but like all such emo-*
> *tional voices, admirably suited to the expression of humor,*
> *and of rising from a touching pathos into the most stirring,*
> *thrilling, and triumphant tones.* (Reid, 1956, p. 281)

The elocutionary style thus described is all but lost today. Martin Luther King Jr. could rise to it; sadly, so could Hitler. But in the nineteenth century, when performative oratory was a significant form of both education and entertainment, no one did it better than Edward Everett.

In Everett's oratory loom the shadows of Lucy Clapp, Masters Little and Tileston, Ezekiel and Daniel Webster, William Biglow, Benjamin Abbott, and Levi Frisbie. And deeply embedded in Everett's eloquence is the figure of John Quincy Adams. To a young and impressionable student, Adams was an unimpeachable source of wisdom. In his afternoon practice sessions, Everett would write and deliver his compositions exactly as he had been taught. As a result, when he graduated from Harvard University in 1811, he was the embodiment of John Quincy Adams's Lectures on Rhetoric and Oratory, his soul burning *with the fires of honorable ambition* to lead his country.

OTHER INFLUENCES ON EDWARD EVERETT'S ORATORY

Everett acknowledged the influence of Benjamin Franklin, who, through his writings, taught the orator the virtues of balance, moderation, and proportion in both his life and his public speaking. *Few books [Franklin's Autobiography] that I have ever read,* Everett noted,

> *had a greater influence on me. I learned from it the supe-*
> *riority of a modest intimation of opinion over dogmatic*
> *assertion and the propriety of speaking with diffidence on*
> *controverted points.* (Reid, 1990, p. 13)

The Orator:
Edward Everett

Franklin's impact on Everett is perhaps best seen in the conciliatory rhetoric of Everett's speeches on the issues of the day, particularly slavery. Even in his Gettysburg Address, as we will see, Everett held out hope that once the radicals were overcome, calmer heads in the South would negotiate the reconstruction of the Union. As noted above, Everett was well acquainted with the speeches of Edmund Burke and Samuel Johnson on England's relations with America prior to the Revolutionary War, and these great orations, he notes in the preface to his Orations and Speeches, reinforced for him the rhetorical techniques necessary to arguing persuasively for either conciliation or forced subservience (1:vii).

We will see in chapter 3 the enormous influence of George Washington and Oliver Everett, Edward's father, on the themes of Edward's oratory and, indeed, on his life. Everett's devotion to the cause of Union and his lifelong concern with the rise of party factionalism after the election of Andrew Jackson are triggered in his earliest boyhood experiences.

Daniel Webster was Everett's closest and lifelong friend, the two having met when they were boys (Webster the older of the two and Everett's mentor) in Ezekiel Webster's school. Daniel Webster's politics would become the basis upon which Everett would form his own, and Webster's fabled eloquence on the floor of the United States Senate would inspire, empower, and challenge Everett. While Everett would break with Webster over the Fugitive Slave Law, Everett would never say so publicly, and his political oratory would continue to reflect his friend's ideas despite the rift.

Through his education in rhetoric and oratory beginning at the age of three; through his life's experiences which, as we have seen, were unparalleled for most Americans of his time; and through his voracious and lifelong appetite for scholarship, Edward Everett would become, as his friend Robert C. Winthrop described him, *our American Cicero*. We turn now to the oratory of Edward Everett, watching him put into practice all that he experienced and all that he had learned about the art of oratory. We will see him become *The Cicero of America*.

WORKS CITED

Adams, John Quincy. Lectures on Rhetoric and Oratory (1810).
Reprint, 2 Vols. Delmar, N.Y.

Ayres, Linda, *Their Unfailing Friend: Edward Everett and the
Mount Vernon Ladies Association* Paper presented at the
annual George Washington Symposium, Mount Vernon,
Virginia, November 8, 2003.

Bode, Carl. The American Lyceum: Town Meeting of the Mind.
New York: Oxford
University Press, 1956.

Brewer, David, ed. The World's Best Orations. 11 Vols, St. Louis
and Chicago: Ferd P. Kaiser, 1899.

Casper, Scott. Constructing American Lives. Chapel Hill: University
of North Carolina Press, 1999.

Clarke, Gregory, and S. Michael Halloran, eds. Oratorical Culture in
Nineteenth-Century America: Transformations in the Theory
and Practice of Rhetoric. Carbondale Southern Illinois
University Press, 1993.

Everett, Edward. Orations and Speeches. 2nd Ed. 2 Vols. Boston:
Little and Brown, 1850.

Frothingham, Paul Revere. Edward Everett: Orator and Statesman.
Boston: Houghton Mifflin Company, 1925.

Kennedy, George. The Art of Persuasion in Greece. Princeton:
Princeton University Press, 1963.

Murphy, James J., and Richard A. Katula. A Synoptic History of Classical Rhetoric. 3rd ed. Mahwah, N.J.: Lawrence Erlbaum Associates, 2003.

Nason, Elias. Tribute to the Memory of Edward Everett by the New England HistoricGenealogical Society. Boston: New England Historic-Genealogical Society, 1895.

Ray, Angela G. The Lyceum and Public Culture in the Nineteenth-Century United States. East Lansing: Michigan State University Press, 1997.

Reid, Ronald, *Edward Everett: Rhetorician of Nationalism,* 1824-1855, Quarterly Journal of Speech 4 (1956): 239-57.

Reid, Ronald. Edward Everett: Unionist Orator. New York: Greenwood Press, 1990.

Smith, Page. The Nation Comes of Age, 8 vols, 1989. NY: McGrawHill, 1981.

Stebbins, Rufus, *Edward Everett as an Orator,* Cornell Era, January 12, 1872, pp. 195-98.

Varg, Paul. Edward Everett: The Intellectual in the Turmoil of Politics. London and
Toronto: Associated University Presses, 1992.

Wills, Garry. Lincoln at Gettysburg: The Words That Remade America. NY: Simon and Schuster, 1992.

3

Edward Everett:
The Cicero of America

> *I do maintain that the complete and perfect orator is he who*
> *can speak about all subjects with fullness and variety.*
> —*Cicero, De Oratore,* I.59

THE ELOQUENCE OF EDWARD EVERETT

No statement more accurately describes Edward Everett than this
one, written by the incomparable Roman orator-statesman Cicero.
In addition to his rhetorical theories, which, as we have seen, had an
enormous influence on the study of rhetoric and oratory in the nineteenth century, Cicero's oratorical practices eclipsed those of his contemporaries so fully that it may be said without hyperbole that they
were engaging in *Ciceronian* rhetoric. Beyond his own time, Cicero's
writings on ethics, politics, and rhetoric suffused the modern age
with its commitment to republican humanism. The first rule of this
humanism, Cicero believed, was that all human beings were born with
a spark of divinity in them —— in a sense *morality* — and were thus
connected to God and to one another in a universal Brotherhood of
Man. (Grant, p. 8-9) For Cicero, the citizen trained in oratory, politics,

and philosophy is charged with putting these divinely inspired moral principles into practice in the conduct of human affairs. *Men excel animals only by having the power of speech,* Cicero asserted, *and the person who excels others in the capacity for eloquence will surely achieve preeminence* (Murphy and Katula, p. 159).

Just as Cicero's extant writings on rhetoric, (8 books, 774 letters, and 58 speeches) and his disciple Quintilian's twelvevolume, Institutio de Oratoria, so deeply affected the founders, so also did they reach into that first generation of Americans, those of the post-founding period who were trained in classical rhetoric by the likes of John Quincy Adams and Joseph McKean. And in no other figure is the imprint of Cicero as profound as in Edward Everett. As we will see, it is little wonder that Everett came to be known as *our Cicero,* or the *Cicero of America,* a man who combined dual careers in letters and politics with a celebrated career as a professional public speaker.

Everett's speeches may be divided into all the varieties of oratory referred to by Adams as demonstrative: lectures, festival orations (such as memorials and dedications), and eulogies. Exactly how many of each genre Everett delivered is difficult to determine, but it is a remarkable list numbering in the hundreds (Appendix A lists all of Everett's public orations as compiled from the 12th edition of his four volume *Orations and Speeches*, Little, Brown, and Company, 1990). At times, Everett would repeat a lecture to accommodate overflow crowds; on other occasions, as many as fifteen to twenty thousand people heard him speak—and heard him, in an age before electronic amplification, as clearly as though he were standing next to them. By the end of his life, Everett's collected orations filled four volumes. He was, indeed, the consummate nineteenth century orator, eclipsing all of his peers in both quantity and quality.

It is not possible to re-create the experience of an Everett oration completely for we cannot capture his stately tones or feel the audience's anticipation as he enters the room or rises to speak. Sad it is for us that technology had not advanced far enough during his lifetime to capture this unique voice for posterity. We do have photographs and portraits, however, and by referring to the vivid descriptions bequeathed to us by those who were in attendance, we can imagine attending an Everett oration and feeling the excitement brought on by his presence. Through reading passages from his orations, we can also appreciate the beauty of the English language as he used it. Most important, by using Adams's lectures as our guide, we can trace how Everett transformed the principles he had learned from his distinguished teacher into pure eloquence. In this chapter, I will do just that, looking at his most famous *lecture*, the aforementioned Phi Beta Kappa Society oration delivered at Harvard University in 1824, entitled *The Circumstances Favorable to the Progress of Literature in America*; a typical patriotic *festival oration*, delivered on the Fourth of July 1833 in Worcester, Massachusetts, and known as *The Seven Years War, The School of the Revolution*; a notable *eulogy*, that for his teacher John Quincy Adams, delivered in 1848; and his most famous *memorial address, The Character of Washington,* delivered 137 times across a four-year period from 1856 to 1860. In the next chapter, I will review in detail his much overlooked and often mischaracterized *dedication speech, The Gettysburg Address,* delivered on November 19, 1863.[17]

Because great orations are often surrounded by larger stories, I will also contextualize my analyses of Everett's oratory with the events that brought them to life and the reactions that followed their performance. In all, we will see in the eloquence of Edward Everett the unique way in which he applied all that he believed, all that he had learned, and all that he had experienced to the shaping of a nation.

The Circumstances Favorable to the Progress of Literature in America, August 26, 1824

Edward Everett's career as an orator began on April 12, 1815, with his inaugural address as Professor of Greek Language and Literature at Harvard University. During the next eight years, he studied in Europe (four years), returned to his teaching post at Harvard, and

---

17. The manuscripts in this chapter and in chapter 4 are available at the website, www.AmericanLyceum.neu.edu. Click on the Readings link and the files will appear under *Edward Everett manuscripts.*

Edward Everett, circa 1850

served as editor of the *North American Review*, and leader of the Greek Revival movement. He ventured onto the public platform for the first time in 1822, when he presented a year-long series of fifteen lectures for the Boston Mercantile Association entitled *Antiquities and Ancient Art*. They were hugely successful, attracting large audiences of Boston's elite, and Everett repeated them for the general public between 1823 and 1824.

On December 19, 1823, he delivered a compelling lecture in Boston urging America's support for Greece in its war to secure its independence from Turkey. The speech was based upon an essay Everett had written earlier that year for the October issue of the North American Review. The speech was a rousing success, and it attracted the attention of Daniel Webster, who made Everett's case to President James Monroe. Had the timing of Everett's speech not coincided with Monroe's State of the Union address that year, the speech in which he introduced his isolationist foreign policy, the Monroe Doctrine, American soldiers may well have been committed to the Greek War of Independence. But such are the vicissitudes of history. Everett remains, in any case, a heroic figure in Greece, his portrait hanging in the National History museum in Athens.

By 1824, Everett had become a public speaker of some note in New England and a commentator of national repute for his essays in the Review. In many of these he gave voice to his belief that America was ripe for the development of its own distinct character. He encouraged Americans to begin to write their own story. Then, in July 1824, a transformational moment for Everett and America, he was invited to present the distinguished Phi Beta Kappa Society oration at Harvard University.

One week prior to the event, which otherwise might have been primarily a gathering of Harvard elites, it was announced that none other than the heroic revolutionary war figure, the Marquis de Lafayette, would be in attendance while passing through Boston on his way to visit the grave of his compatriot George Washington. Public excitement grew, the room now filled to capacity, and necks craned through the church windows as eyes struggled to catch a glimpse of France's American Revolutionary war hero. The Reverend Henry Ware Jr., a notable Unitarian minister, welcomed the audience with a moving poem. Everett then made his appearance on the platform. The aforementioned Rufus Stebbins described the moment this way:

> *Mr. Everett came forward in the full glow of manly beauty...*
> *and standing out upon the platform, without any manu-*
> *script or brief in his hand commenced in clear, untremu-*
> *lous and silvery tones his oration upon the Circumstances*
> *Favorable to the Progress of Literature in America. He*
> *sketched with inimitable grace and graphicness the fields*
> *open for the ambitious—broad as our prairies, grand as*
> *our lakes and cataracts, stirring as our colonial history*
> *and revolutionary struggles, of which he gave some brilliant*
> *pictures. The sympathies of the vast audience kindled as the*
> *form of the orator expanded and his face glowed with the*
> *increasing interest of his theme. As he approached his grand*
> *climax, the whole audience were of one countenance, thrilled*
> *with one emotion. It was a grand musical instrument,*
> *every string responding to the skillful touch of the orator.*
> (Stebbins, p. 196)

Delivering his speech from memory, Everett adapted his remarks brilliantly to the expanded purpose of the occasion: freed from its English roots, separated by a vast ocean, and blessed with unbounded natural resources, America was now in a unique position to write its own history, develop its own traditions, and establish its own identity. He framed the central idea, the *state of the controversy,* in his exordium:

> *On this occasion, it has seemed proper to me that we should*
> *turn our thoughts, not merely to some topic of literary inter-*
> *est, but to one which concerns us as American scholars. I*
> *have accordingly selected, as the subject of our inquiry, the*
> *circumstances favorable to the progress of literature in the*
> *United States of America. In the discussion of this subject,*
> *that curiosity, which every scholar naturally feels, in trac-*
> *ing and comparing the character of the higher civilization of*
> *different countries, is at once dignified and rendered practi-*
> *cal by the connection of the inquiry with the condition and*
> *prospects of his native land.*

> *... These topics of national curiosity and liberal speculation ... acquire practical importance when the land in which we ourselves live is the subject of investigation. When we turn to the inquiry of our own country; when we survey its natural features, search its history, and examine its institutions, to see what are the circumstances which are to excite and guide the popular mind, it then becomes an inquiry of the highest interest, and worthy of the attention of every patriotic scholar. We then dwell, not on a distant, uncertain, fabulous past, but on an impending future, teeming with individual and public fortune; a future, toward which we are daily and rapidly moving forward, and with which we stand in the dearest connection that can bind the generations of men together; a future, which our own characters, actions, and principles, may influence for good or evil, for lasting glory or shame. We then strive, as far as our poor philosophy can do it, to read the country's reverend auspices; to cast its great horoscope in the national sky, where some stars are waning, and some have set. We endeavor to ascertain whether the soil, which we love as that where our fathers are laid, and we shall presently be laid with them, is likely to be trod, in times to come, by an enlightened, virtuous, and free people.*

Moving to his narrative, Everett noted that those circumstances favorable to the progress of literature in America were three in number: (1) a populist democracy governed by a Constitution rather than a king; (2) a common culture spread across a vast expanse of geography and united by one language; and (3) a swelling population moving west and creating unbounded experiences about which to write. These dynamic conditions, when contrasted with Europe's entrenched customs and bureaucracies, point America irreversibly in one direction: forward. Here was a blank canvas upon which the American scholar could sketch, were he so inclined, the images of ordinary people living a uniquely American experience, and out of this effort would emerge an American tradition in literature and the arts.

For the next hour, Everett supported his arguments with compelling logic. A free system of representative government was a more natural state for humanity than monarchical forms, he reasoned, for each citizen came to feel *the consciousness of his own social importance.* In addition, because language barriers did not exist across regions of the United States, misunderstandings such as those that led to conflict in Europe were more easily avoided. Finally, the rapid growth of the American population, compared to the declining population of many European countries, would inevitably increase America's influence in world trade.

Western civilization, he observed, has always moved westward, from Greece, to Rome, to England, and then across the Atlantic ocean to America. Now, he noted,

> *There are no more continents to be revealed; Atlantis hath arisen from the ocean; the farthest Thule is reached; there are no more retreats beyond the sea, no more discoveries, no more hopes. Here, then, a mighty work is to be performed, or never, by mortals.... Yes, brethren, it is by the intellect of the country that the mighty mass is to be inspired; that its parts are to communicate and sympathize with each other; its natural progress to be adorned with becoming refinements; its principles asserted and its feelings interpreted to its own children, to other regions, and to after ages.*

Should anyone remain still doubtful of his prospectus, Everett invoked the guidance of Divine Providence:

> *This, then, is the theatre on which the intellect of America is to appear, and such the motives of its exertion; such the mass to be influenced by its energies; such the glory to crown its success. If I err in this happy vision of my country's fortunes, I thank Heaven for an error so animating. Never may you, my friends, be under any other feeling, than that a great, a growing, an immeasurably expanding country is calling upon you for your best services.*

... One might almost think, without extravagance, that the departed wise and good, of all places and times, are looking down from their happy seats to witness what shall now be done by us; that they who lavished their treasures and their blood, who spoke and wrote, who labored, fought, and perished in the one great cause of Freedom and Truth, are now hanging their orbs on high, over the last solemn experiment of humanity.

All the while, sitting immediately to Everett's right as though bearing witness to the orator's prophecy, was one of those great men *to whom, under Providence,* Everett noted, *we owe our existence*: the Marquis de Lafayette. The celebrated Frenchman had actually understood very little of what Everett had just said, but he had enthusiastically joined the audience in continuous applause. After one hour, Everett reached his peroration, and, sensing the sentimental possibilities inherent in the moment, he turned to the celebrated Frenchman and addressed him directly:

Welcome, friend of our fathers to our shores! Happy are our eyes that behold those venerable features! Enjoy a triumph such as never conqueror nor monarch enjoyed— the assurance that, throughout America, there is not a bosom which does not beat with joy and gratitude at the sound of your name! You have already met and saluted, or will soon meet, the few that remain of the ardent patriots, prudent counselors, and brave warriors with whom you were associated in achieving our liberty. But you have looked round in vain for the faces of many, who would have lived years of pleasure on a day like this, with their old companion in arms and brothers in peril.... Above all, the first of heroes and of men, the friend of your youth, the more than friend of his country, rests in the bosom of the soil he redeemed. On the banks of his Potomac he lies in glory and peace. You will revisit the hospitable shades of Mount Vernon, but him, whom you venerated

> *as we did, you will not meet at its door.... But the grateful*
> *children of America will bid you welcome in his name. And*
> *withersoever your course shall take you, throughout the lim-*
> *its of this continent, the ear that hears you shall bless you, the*
> *eye that sees you shall give witness to you, and every tongue*
> *proclaim, with heartfelt joy, Welcome! Thrice welcome*
> *LaFayette, to our shores.*

The hyperbole was perfect. The address could not have reached a more appropriately sentimental crescendo. Those in attendance cheered; they waved their handkerchiefs; they wept. Reverend Ware wrote to his mother that

> *Everett's address was very fine. The concluding address to*
> *Lafayette was one of the most affecting and overpowering*
> *efforts of eloquence I ever witnessed; it shook the whole audi-*
> *ence, and bathed every face in tears. When he sat down, it*
> *was followed with nine cheers in an interminable clapping.*
> (Varg, p. 29)

Newspapers accounts of the speech were uniformly positive. One, that in the Boston Commercial Gazette, (30 August, 1824), captured the reigning opinion:

> *The Oration, by Professor Everett, was learned, elaborate,*
> *excursive, and tasteful; abounding with deep thought, bold*
> *principles, and striking illustrations. This writer seems to*
> *come with wizard power, and the materials of the ancient*
> *and modern temples of learning are dismembered in the spell,*
> *and a new edifice of his own is erected, combining the beau-*
> *ties of every order. The address to Lafayette was delicate*
> *and affectionate, and the effects on the audience wonderful.*
> *There were some lion-hearts, and others, as cold as icebergs,*
> *that melted at his appeal.* (p. 3).

Perhaps most notably, as his mentor John Quincy Adams had taught him, Everett had *ascertained precisely the state of the controversy.* He had seized the moment and bent it to his purpose. Further, with his repetition of the words *inquiry* and *future* in his exordium, he had shaped the event's mood. From the outset, the speech was optimistic, idealistic, and forward looking—youthful, energetic rhetoric for a youthful, energetic nation awakening to its distinctive opportunities. Everett had accomplished the essential aim of the lecture format: to meditate on possibilities and to increase adherence to the values upon which a realization of those possibilities would be built: liberty and popular government, freedom and truth. These, he noted, would *give elevation, dignity, and generous expansion to every species of mental effort.* His praise for Lafayette had simply given license to the passions waiting to explode in the audience.

The speech remains today a masterpiece of erudition, roaming widely for allusions, as it does, through the ages of the Egyptian, Greek, Roman, and English empires. Everett sprinkled his address with quotations, including stanzas of poetry from Milton and Latinate expressions from the Roman historian Tacitus. Through this *lackering of language,* as Adams had called it, Everett provided a scholarly meditation on political sociology perfectly suited in style and substance for the oldest honor society in the United States, the Phi Beta Kappa Society.

The oration is a banquet of figurative expressions, those artful deviations from the ordinary meaning of a word or the ordinary construction of a sentence that are used to give clarity and/or adornment to an address. In the few excerpts above, for instance, we find epanaphora, metaphor, metonymy, hyperbole, and personification. Taking just one of these, epanaphora, we see how a word, when repeated, can compact and hold together a series of clauses and give emphasis to key ideas. In his exordium, for example, Everett uses epanaphora to sharpen the focus on the collective effort he urges on his audience: when we turn to our country, and we dwell on it, and we strive to understand it, and we endeavor to ascertain its future, we find that we are launched on a great experiment. Or later, when detailing the role of the scholar in America, Everett's message is precise: the country's intellectuals will survey its parts, its natural progress, its principles, its feelings, and they will interpret these to its children, to other regions, and to other ages. This rhetorical technique keeps the energy level high and the focus intact throughout the one-hour address. In short, by using such rhetorical techniques, the orator amplifies his ideas in the very manner Adams had advised (2:236-38).

The lecture is replete with metaphors that compare America to a theatre and metonyms[18] that cast Europe as the *Old World*. Figures such as these transfer the meaning or connotation from the noun used to the noun specified through simple, we might say archetypal, comparisons such as *new* versus *old*. Also noticeable in Everett's peroration to Lafayette is the evocation of the senses (the ear, the eye, the tongue), a rhetorical technique right out of Adams's playbook. Although the copious use of figures and imagery lends the address a florid quality, that characteristic is not inappropriate to the dignity of a Phi Beta Kappa Society oration at the nation's most distinguished university, Harvard. The style, in other words, matches the occasion, and Everett's figures illuminate rather than overpower. Who else but Cicero himself could have written sentence after sentence with the rhythm and flow of this one:

> *We then strive, as far as our poor philosophy can do it, to read the country's reverend auspices; to cast its great horoscope in the national sky, where some stars are waning, and some have set.*

For Everett, however, the child prodigy grown into the most famous public intellectual of his day, bursts of eloquence such as this were expected and they were delivered.

As Preacher Ware noted, when Everett sat down, the crowd responded with nine hurrahs and endless applause. The object of the nine cheers was Edward Everett as much as it was Lafayette, and the speech would launch Everett into politics. He was quickly nominated

---

18. A figure of speech in which one word is substituted for another in order to provide a connotation.

by the Whig Party for a seat in Congress, and he was quickly endorsed by all political factions, including the Democrat-leaning Boston Courier, for his nonpartisanship, his intellectual acumen, and *the patriotic spirit of the Phi Beta Kappa oration* (Reid, 1990, p. 27). Elected by an overwhelming margin, Everett set out in January 1826 for Washington, D.C., and a new career in politics.

THE SEVEN YEARS WAR; THE SCHOOL OF THE REVOLUTION, JULY 4, 1833

Edward Everett's ten years in Congress were a disappointment, even to him, for reasons already mentioned. He was, nevertheless, throughout the years from 1826 to 1835, a sought after speaker. His unique voice and sophisticated presence made him the *complete and perfect orator* for any public gathering requiring a moment of eloquence. In particular, Everett became a popular festival orator, the first choice for commemorative events, national anniversary addresses, eulogies, and lectures. He was ubiquitous at lyceums, and he delivered Fourth of July orations in towns throughout Massachusetts. He spoke on a wide range of topics, from tariffs, to the nation's founding, to biographies of famous Americans such as Benjamin Franklin. He often spoke to overflow crowds, and on some occasions such as his lecture in Salem on *The Present State and Prospects of Europe,* he agreed to repeat the speech the following evening in order to accommodate those who could not squeeze into the hall. The Christian Examiner captured these years perfectly:

> *Since the Address before the Phi Beta Kappa society in 1824,*
> *there has hardly been any marked occasion or event or man*
> *among us that has not been commemorated by Mr. Everett's*
> *ample and accomplished rhetoric.* (Reid, 1956, p. 273)

Everett's diary suggests that he devoted endless hours during this period to composing and rehearsing his speeches. Despite the length of some—often one to two hours—he declaimed each address from memory. He would sometimes bring to the lectern his entire manuscript, sometimes just a single note card, but these he employed more as props than aids. He reported having had anxiety on some occasions, yet it was never noticeable. He remained animated and spontaneous even when delivering somewhat mundane lectures such as his *Advantages of Scientific Knowledge to Working Men,* which, by popular demand, he repeated five times. And despite having memorized his speeches, they were filled with detail. He viewed a festival oration or a lecture as an occasion to fulfill Cicero's three goals of oratory: to inspire, to delight, to teach. To the ordinary citizens who attended his lyceum lectures or his Fourth of July orations during this period, many of whom had only a modicum of formal schooling, Everett's eloquence was not only moving and patriotic but also educational.

One theme that emerges during this period and continues throughout Everett's career is his hatred of party faction and his devotion to Union. His years in Congress had left him tired and wary of the infighting and political intrigue that polarized every issue. He saw in the Manichean drift into parties and sections the seeds of war. These years reignited a concern and a fear that had been drilled into a very young Edward Everett by his father, Oliver. There is, in fact, a poignant story about the moment Edward Everett became devoted to George Washington's life and legacy; it is a story that also helps us understand Everett's festival oratory; indeed, Edward Everett himself.

It was the 22nd day of February 1800, in the town of Dorchester, Massachusetts. The citizens had gathered to express their grief over the death of George Washington and to give testimonials in his honor. The bell tolled, minute guns were discharged, and an American flag was displayed, at half mast, from the gunhouse. A procession was formed, cannons fired, and speakers assembled at the meeting house to pray for and eulogize the *Father of His Country.* The official duty to deliver the memorial remarks, fateful as it would become, fell to one of Dorchester's leading citizens, Oliver Everett. As he proclaimed *Fellow citizens,* the crowd fell silent. Among those gathered around the stage was a nearly six-year old Edward Everett, the youngest son of the speaker.

Oliver Everett spared not a single superlative or moral approximation in describing Washington's life and the qualities of his character:

> *The ancestors of General Washington were respectable. From them he received a plentiful fortune, and by private tutors a good education. Nature furnished him with a strong, energetic mind, and a heart of keen sensibility. By constant industry, his understanding became stored with useful knowledge, and his temper formed to the most perfect order. His judgment was remarkably correct, yet surprisingly rapid. His integrity was unblemished, his humanity ever conspicuous and his benevolence unbounded. Neither in action, nor in suffering, did his courage or his prudence ever fail. He possessed the moral principle in its most refined state; an undissembled piety dwelt in his heart. From this combination of shining virtues, resulted an undeviating course of right actions, which early gained him the respect and confidence of his fellow-citizens.* (Everett, Oliver, p. 8)

When the nation chose *to be free or to perish,* as Oliver Everett put it, its citizens turned to Washington to lead them to victory. With characteristic modesty, Washington accepted the nation's confidence and proved worthy of it:

> *The prudence of General Washington was equal to his wisdom; and united with an inflexible perseverance, his courage conducted the American armies to a final triumph. The event humbled our adversaries and astonished the world. America rejoiced in her independence and gratefully acknowledged her illustrious Chief to be the author of it. Nothing less than a combination of the wonderful talents which Washington possessed could have brought this revolution to an happy issue. Without an American army, Washington, indeed, could not have conquered. Without a Washington, the American armies would have been defeated.* (pp. 12–13)

Everett's stately antithesis captured a peculiarly fortunate moment for the new nation: when a man and a set of circumstances were perfectly suited one to the other:

> *His wisdom, firmness, and impartiality saved us from the*
> *most imminent dangers, preserved the national dignity, and*
> *secured our neutral situation.* (p. 14)

Washington was, in other words, the embodiment of Aristotle's
golden mean. Everett urged his compatriots to read, if they had
not, and to teach to their children Washington's Farewell Address, a
timeless document that, he said, *has been more universally read and
admired than any other political composition.* He exhorted the crowd:

> *Citizens! Have you perused it? If you have not, suffer not the*
> *disgrace. Purchase it as a valuable relict, study it with atten-*
> *tion, teach it to your children, rehearse it to your friends.*
> (p. 15)

In his stirring and poetic peroration, Everett issued a word of warning to, followed by a sentimental and optimistic prediction about, his
fellow citizens:

> *By far the greatest portion of our citizens, it is believed, are*
> *friends to order and our excellent Constitution. But vast*
> *numbers of these, content themselves with the enjoyment of*
> *Liberty and regard with an eye of indifference the disputes of*
> *professed politicians. But should these rise to a crisis more*
> *imminently dangerous, they will quit their ease, and will*
> *cause their voices to be heard. Should no other means be*
> *found to recall the nation to reason, they will arise; they will*
> *take their beloved offspring by the hand, and march towards*
> *the tomb of Washington. Their numbers will multiply at*
> *every stage. Around the venerable repository of his ashes,*
> *they will extend a circle, large as the eye can ken. On their*
> *bended knee, with their eyes and their hands raised towards*
> *Heaven, they will swear, to preserve from ruin their beloved*
> *country; and to perpetuate those national blessings which it*
> *enjoyed, under the patronage of its departed Saviour. The*
> *effect shall be wonderful. Patriotism shall revive; like the*

electrical flame, it shall rapidly extend throughout the Union.
Faction shall vanish. Order shall return. Righteousness
shall rein. (p. 21)

Oliver Everett's words imprinted themselves on the mind of
young Edward. Some Everett scholars[19] have even gone so far as
to speculate that from this moment, Edward Everett's oratory was
dominated and driven by the themes his father asserted in this eulogy
to Washington. Washington's Farewell Address would become
Everett's polestar, and near the end of his life, he would recall that
day in Dorchester in vivid detail.

Upon the death of General Washington, in 1799, my father
was requested to deliver a Eulogy, on the next 22nd of
February. Father's health had long been feeble. Nothing
but his profound personal veneration for the character of
Washington induced him to make the effort.

Indeed, as it was with me at Gettysburg, so was it then with
him. He found it impossible to refuse—His appearance as a
public speaker for the first time in many years was an event
of the greatest importance in the family. I had only seen him
in the ordinary forms and acts of domestic life.

When the great day came—the whole town, civil and mili-
tary, old and young, male and female, was in motion at an
early hour. The artillery fired minute guns, the light infan-
try paraded, the bell tolled. The galleries of the meetinghouse
were filled with women at an early hour; the men, four com-
panies of infantry, a troop of dismounted cavalry were mar-
shaled without. There was a good deal of marching, counter
marching & delay as always happens on these occasions.
Mourning sashes with a likeness of Washington were worn

---

19. Jim Cooke, the renowned scholar/interpreter of Edward Everett is the
main source of this assertion.

by the ladies & appropriate badges by the men; the juveniles were provided with a sketch on white metal, the head of Washington on one side; and a weeping willow on the other, with the legend, "he is in glory, the world is in tears." The pupils of all the schools who were over seven years formed a part of the procession.

As I was not quite six, I was excluded from the procession, a circumstance however, which procured me the advantage of going into the meetinghouse with my mother, before the exercise commenced. The pulpit was dressed in black, [the cloth] from which my father was afterwards complimented with a suit of clothes. It was later said: "He went about clad in the mantel of his eloquence." A very large choir rehearsed a funeral anthem. The artillery fired every five minutes, and the bell tolled with melancholy assiduity. Had the state of excitement occasioned by these unusual sights and sounds lasted much longer, I could hardly have been able to support it!

I recollect my father's pallid countenance; & the subdued tone with which he began, "Prepare then to hear the words of truth, unadorned with the flowers of eloquence, and uttered with a feeble voice.

Later that day, we had company at dinner, & a reception in the afternoon. In eating a St. Germain pear my two under teeth were loosened. I ran to my father to know what should be done. Placing his thumb in my mouth by way of exploring the premises & perceiving that the mission of the teeth was accomplished, he forced them wholly out,—an event, which to my childish apprehension added considerably to the strange, confused, and bewildering character of the day.

Among the numerous poetical effusions caused by the death of Washington was one of twelve or fourteen lines beginning

> From Vernon's mount behold the hero rise
> Resplendent forms attendant through the skies.

> *This I adopted for declamation and raised my arm—thus*
> *while repeating the first line, "From Vernon's mount behold*
> *the hero rise." I kept it elevated during the whole piece.*[20]

It is natural to wonder what specific ideas from Washington's
Farewell Address would have had such a pronounced effect on a boy
not yet six years old. The address is commonly cited as one of the
most enlightened and important documents in American history. It is,
perhaps, best known for the president's warning to his successors to
avoid *entangling alliances,* a warning that in 1823 would underwrite
the Monroe Doctrine and, for the next two hundred years, American
foreign policy in general. But Washington's address was much
grander than that one issue; it was an encomium, replete with optimism about the nation's future, but tempered with words of caution
and advice to the Union the Constitution had established.

Washington's characteristic modesty and humility are evident in
his exordium, as he ascribes any successes he may have had to the
support of the public:

> *If benefits have resulted to our country from these services, let*
> *it always be remembered to your praise, and as an instruc-*
> *tive example in our annals, that under circumstances in*
> *which the passions, agitated in every direction, were liable*
> *to mislead, amidst appearances sometimes dubious, vicis-*
> *situdes of fortune often discouraging, in situations in which*
> *not unfrequently want of success has countenanced the spirit*
> *of criticism, the constancy of your support was the essential*
> *prop of the efforts, and a guarantee of the plans by which*
> *they were effected.* (Brewer, p. 3742)

---

20. From Jim Cooke's one-man show on Edward Everett. Used by his
suggestion and with his permission.

Here are the words that had animated Oliver Everett's peroration: an unshakeable faith in a vigilant public. A watchful public provides the constancy that guides the country forward and assures its preservation. But Washington also recognizes that the public is susceptible to selfishness and corruption when those twin evils are forged on the anvil of sectional chauvinism. In a prescient moment, Washington exhorts his fellow countrymen to place the interests of the Union above their own:

> *The unity of government which constitutes you one people is also now dear to you. It is justly so, for it is a main pillar in the edifice of your real independence, the support of your tranquility at home, your peace abroad; of your safety; of your prosperity; of that very liberty which you so highly prize. But as it is easy to foresee that, from different causes and from different quarters, much pains will be taken, many artifices employed to weaken in your minds the conviction of this truth; as this is the point of your political fortress against which the batteries of internal and external enemies will be most constantly and actively directed (though often covertly and insidiously) directed, it is of infinite moment that you should properly estimate the immense value of your national union to your collective and individual happiness.*
> (Brewer, p. 3743)

The name *America*, Washington declares, *must always exalt the just pride of patriotism more than any appellation derived from local discriminations.* Washington is particularly concerned with the withering effects on the Union of party faction.

> *The common and continual mischiefs of the spirit of party are sufficient to make it the interest and duty of a wise people to discourage and restrain it.* (Brewer, p. 3748)

In similar measure, Washington urges the public to adhere to other values upon which he believes a free people must govern itself. First, to preserve constitutional government, the three branches of government must honor the principle of checks and balances. Further, religion and morality must be respected as an indispensable foundation for popular government. Finally, education, or what Washington calls *institutions for the general diffusion of knowledge,* must be supported and continually strengthened so that the public might remain adequately informed.

Washington then turns to his better-known remarks on foreign policy. He exhorts the nation to *observe good faith and justice towards all nations; cultivate peace and harmony.* Favor no nation over another, he argues, regardless of past history. *Harmony, liberal intercourse with all nations, are recommended by policy, humanity, and interest* (Brewer, p. 3753). Having sounded this cautionary note, Washington departs the scene with what is one of the most modest and humble perorations in American presidential history:

> *Though, in reviewing the incidents of my administration, I am unconscious of intentional error, I am nevertheless too sensible of my defects not to think it probable that I may have committed many errors. Whatever they may be, I fervently beseech the Almighty to avert or mitigate the evils to which they may tend. I shall also carry with me the hope that my country will never cease to view them with indulgence; and that, after forty-five years of my life dedicated to its services with an upright zeal, the faults of incompetent abilities will be consigned to oblivion, as myself must soon be to the mansions of rest.* (Brewer, p. 3755)

Washington's Farewell Address displays the virtues characteristic of him: justice, courage, perseverance, modesty, humility, and political magnanimity. For a nation setting out to establish its identity, construct its myths and heroes, and engrave in words the political principles that would govern its fate, there was no better text than this one, Oliver and Edward Everett believed, and no better American than George Washington.

Edward Everett embraced Washington's words wholeheartedly. The great general's patriotism, idealism, and optimism, coupled with his belief in harmony and conciliation among political parties and with other nations, would inform Everett's politics and his oratory for the rest of his life. As we will see, Everett's most famous speech, *The Character of Washington,* derives much of its inspiration from Washington's Farewell Address and Oliver Everett's eulogy. It was during his waning years in Congress, however, that Everett became especially devoted to this theme, and there is, perhaps, no better example of that commitment to Union than his Fourth of July oration delivered in Worcester, Massachusetts, in 1833. The address is known as *The Seven Years War; The School of the Revolution.*

Everett reports that he composed and rehearsed the speech for a number of days and on some (such as 27–29 June) for most of the day (Papers, Vol. 36, 146). He arrived in Worcester early on the morning of July 4th to survey the scene, and around 8:30 A.M., he looked into the church where he would speak. It was already filled to capacity. A short time later, he addressed the citizens of Worcester for one hour and a quarter.

The exordium is classic in its composition, generating good will through Everett's characteristic modesty and with references to the occasion itself.

> *I have accepted with great cheerfulness the invitation with which you have honored me to address you on this occasion. The citizens of Worcester did not wait to receive a second call before they hastened to the relief of the citizens of Middlesex in the times that tried men's souls. I should feel myself degenerate and unworthy, could I hesitate to come, and, in my humble measure, assist you in commemorating those exploits which your fathers so promptly and so nobly aided our fathers in achieving.*

He then extends the exordium through digression (a common Ciceronian technique advocated by Adams), taking advantage of the fact that the invitation was endorsed by the citizenry of Worcester without distinction of party. Herein lay an opportunity, and he presses his case.

In fact, fellow citizens, I deem it one of the happiest effects of the celebration of this anniversary, that, when undertaken in the spirit which has animated you on this occasion it has the natural tendency to soften the harshness of party, which I cannot but regard as the great bane of our prosperity. It was pronounced by Washington, in his valedictory address to the people of the United States, "the worst enemy of popular governments"; and the experience of almost every administration, from his own down, has confirmed the truth of the remark. The spirit of party unquestionably has its source in some native passions of the heart; and free governments naturally furnish more of its aliment than those under which the liberty of speech and of the press is restrained by the strong arm of power. But, so naturally does party run into extremes,—so unjust, cruel, and remorseless is it in its excess,—so ruthless in the war which it wages against private character,—so unscrupulous in the choice of means for the attainment of selfish ends,—so sure is it, eventually, to dig the grave of those free institutions,—so inevitably does it end in military despotism and unmitigated tyranny, that I do not know how the voice and influence of a good man could, with more propriety, be exerted, than in the effort to assuage its violence....

Far distant be all of these inauspicious calculations. It is the natural tendency of celebrating the fourth of July, to strengthen the sentiment of attachment to the Union. It carries us back to other days of yet greater peril to our beloved country, when a still stronger bond of feeling and action united the hearts of her children. It recalls to us the sacrifices of those who deserted the walks of private industry, and abandoned the prospects of opening life, to engage in the service of their country.... It calls up, as it were, from the beds of glory and peace where they lie,—from the heights of Charlestown to the southern plains,—the vast and venerable congregation of those who bled in the sacred cause. They

> *gather in saddened majesty around us, and adjure us, by*
> *their returning agonies and re-opening wounds, not to per-*
> *mit our feuds and dissensions to destroy the value of that*
> *birthright which they purchased with their precious lives.*

We read here a precise and emphatic affirmation of Everett's devotion to the cause of Union. Just as he had adapted to Lafayette's presence with his Phi Beta Kappa Society oration, Everett seized on the language of the invitation from Worcester to drive home his exhortation. No one could be offended, and no expression of patriotism could be more appropriate for this occasion. The orator has found in an act of his audience, their invitation to him, the very idea he may use to increase their adherence to the values embodied in the event itself.

The central idea of the speech, the state of the controversy, is that the exigencies of colonial life had delivered a civil and military education that had prepared the colonists for their later push toward independence. Everett finds the causal train compelling:

> *My object has merely been to point out the curious historical*
> *connection between the consolidation and the downfall of*
> *the British Empire in America, consequent upon the success-*
> *ful issue of the Seven Years' War. One consequence only may*
> *deserve to be specified, of a different character, but spring-*
> *ing from the same source, and tending to the same end, and*
> *more decisive of the fate of the revolution than any other*
> *merely political circumstance. The event which wrested her*
> *colonial possessions on this continent from France, gave to*
> *our fathers a friend in that power which had hitherto been*
> *their most dreaded enemy, and prepared France,—by the*
> *gradual operation of public sentiment, and the influence of*
> *reasons of state,—when the accepted time should arrive, to*
> *extend to them an efficient hand to aid them in establishing*
> *their independence.*

Everett's ensuing narrative is a history lesson of the Seven Years War (1754–63), which was led by Colonel George Washington against the French and the Indians. Everett admits that a festival oration should contain more of *the effusion of kind and patriotic feeling than of labored discussion,* but with a brief apology, he justifies his extended use of the lecture format. The Seven Years War set the stage, he argues, for the Declaration of Independence, and so this historical prelude prepares the audience for the essential object of his Fourth of July address.

Even while making his case, Everett is conciliatory toward England, noting that although the greatest incident of America's young life was breaking free of king and Parliament, there are, nevertheless, *many ties which ought to bind our feelings to the land of our fathers.* In an otherwise unfriendly review of British-American relations, Everett asks,

> *Where are the graves of our Fathers? In England. The school of the free principles, in which, as the last great lesson, the doctrine of our independence was learned, where did it subsist? In the hereditary love of liberty of the Anglo-Saxon race.*

By this point in his oration, Everett has accomplished his two purposes: a patriotic exhortation on the virtues of the Union, followed by an acknowledgment of the nation's English origins. Both ideas come directly from Washington's Farewell Address, deriving their ethos from this great American as much as from Everett himself.

The style of the address is appropriately mixed, shifting from a highly figurative and poetic exordium to a more prosaic history lecture of the narrative. This fusion of pathos and logos, so characteristic of Cicero's oratory, becomes Everett's way of moving from inspiration to education and back again.

As he had with his Phi Beta Kappa Society oration, Everett uses a bounty of figurative expressions to impress his audience with the gravity of the event. He uses, as he did in Cambridge, the figure of epanaphora to hold his auditors' attention and to emphasize his disgust for party faction:

> *so naturally does party run into extremes,—so unjust, cruel,*
> *and remorseless is it in its excess,—so ruthless in the war*
> *which it wages against private character,—so unscrupu-*
> *lous in the choice of means for the attainment of selfish*
> *ends,—so sure is it, eventually, to dig the grave of those free*
> *institutions,—so inevitably does it end in military despotism*
> *and unmitigated tyranny, that I do not know how the voice*
> *and influence of a good man could, with more propriety, be*
> *exerted, than in the effort to assuage its violence....*

Early in the exordium, to generate the sentimental, patriotic mood
he desires, Everett alludes to *the times that tried men's souls,* from
Thomas Paine's inspiring Revolutionary-era pamphlet The Crisis.
Understanding the nature of his audience in Worcester, Everett recalls
a tract designed to help ordinary citizens understand the need to
separate from England. His metaphor *school of free principles,* which
he employs to describe England, also illustrates the skill with which
Everett uses language to capture his exact thought; that is, England is
no longer an enemy but a lesson in government for America.

In his peroration, Everett pulls the discourse together with the same
optimism that characterized his address to the Phi Beta Kappa Society:

> *With the result of our happily organized liberty we are start-*
> *ing, fellow citizens, on the second half-century since the close*
> *of the revolutionary war. Let us hope that we are to move*
> *with a still accelerated pace on the path of improvement and*
> *happiness, of public and private virtue and honor. When*
> *we compare what our beloved country now is,—or, to go*
> *no further than our own states, when we compare what*
> *Massachusetts now is with what it was fifty years ago,—what*
> *grounds for honest pride and boundless gratitude does not*
> *the comparison suggest!*

The oration, brimming as it was with patriotic, optimistic, and conciliatory rhetoric, brought cheers from Everett's audience and acclaim from
the press. The Worcester Spy, (July 11, 1833) for example, wrote that

Of the oration, we hardly dare ourselves to speak, lest we should be thought to exaggerate its merits; but to those who have ever heard Edward Everett on such an occasion, we need only say that he equaled his usual efforts. He spoke, without the use of even the briefest notes, for one hour and ten minutes, in a style of eloquence that completely riveted the attention of the vast assembly before him. He took his position upon the stage, in a plain dress and poured forth the treasure of a highly cultivated mind, and a well-stored memory, in such a manner as to elicit frequent bursts of applause from the audience. (Papers, 50: 249)

The writer then added,

The celebration of the 4th of July at Worcester was the most brilliant intellectual exhibition made in the Commonwealth on that day. It was the union of all parties upon Republican principles. (Papers, Vol. 50: 249)

Praise for Everett's oratory, much of it like that quoted above, prompted appeals that he run for governor of Massachusetts. On March 4, 1835, he was nominated by both the Anti-Masonic Party and the Whig Party; he was easily elected on November 9, 1835, by a vote of more than two to one. He served as governor for four years.

Everett was well suited for the role. As Frothingham notes, he was dignified, courteous, able, upright, fond of ceremony, tireless in attention to detail, a conscientious public servant, and with no rival as an orator except Daniel Webster and possibly Rufus Choate. (p. 129)

And despite the crush of obligations and the heartbreaking death of his daughter, Grace Fletcher, Everett continued to accept speaking engagements. Just days after his election, he delivered two public lectures sponsored by the Massachusetts Historical Society, one on the Peruvian Indians and one on the Mexican Indians. He repeated both lectures to lyceum audiences soon thereafter. For the rest of the decade and throughout his tenure as governor, he gave numerous after-dinner speeches as well as lectures at lyceums and to various professional associations across Massachusetts. His topics ranged from improvements to the prison system to public education, economics, and patriotism. He also delivered a number of eulogies to departed dignitaries. His diary entries suggest that he delighted in every occasion that brought him to the platform.

One topic Everett did not address while governor, except in his initial statement (his inaugural address) to a joint session of the Massachusetts legislature, was slavery. His remarks on this occasion were as poorly received as his speech in the United States Congress had been ten years earlier. Everett noted that slavery, while *held in public estimation as an evil of the first magnitude* in Massachusetts, had been upheld by all parties during the process of ratifying the Constitution. He asked that a *veil of silence* now be imposed on the topic:

> *The patriotism of all classes of citizens must be invoked to abstain from a discussion, which, by exasperating the master, can have no other effect than to render more oppressive the condition of the slave, and which, if not abandoned, there is great reason to fear, will prove the rock on which the Union will split.*

He argued that the issue should be left alone until,

> *Providence, who, in his own good time is able to cause it to disappear like the slavery of the ancient world under the gradual operation of the gentle spirit of Christianity.*
> (Frothingham, p. 132)

Everett's sentiments accorded with those of the majority of citizens in Massachusetts, and they reflected his lifelong concern for sectional faction. Given that Massachusetts was the site of the abolitionist movement, however, and that in 1836 the movement had crescendoed, Everett's words were met with scorn. James Russell Lowell, a distinguished citizen of the commonwealth and ardent abolitionist, put it best:

> *To be told that we ought not to agitate the question of slavery, when it is that which forever is agitating us, is like telling a man with fever and ague on him to stop shaking and he will be cured.* (Frothingham, p. 133)

Chastened by such responses, Everett imposed a veil of silence on himself concerning the divisive topic of slavery for the rest of his tenure as governor.

Everett's years as minister to England were also punctuated with speaking engagements. His reputation as a gifted orator preceded him to the Court of Saint James', and throughout 1842 and 1843, he offered speeches, mostly of the after-dinner variety, at a string of universities and societies.

Upon returning to the United States and assuming the presidency of Harvard University, Everett took up the cause of the Irish famine, and in 1847 he spoke on behalf of its victims at three separate fundraising events. Then, on April 25, 1848, at the unanimous request of the Massachusetts legislature, Everett was invited to deliver the commonwealth's main eulogy to his recently departed (February 23, 1848) teacher, dear friend, and former president of the United States, John Quincy Adams.

Everett immediately accepted the invitation. He worked on the speech daily, writing in his diary of the constant interruptions he endured from students, faculty, and trustees at Harvard, intrusions that, he complained, *consume all of my time, sweat, and my life* (Papers, 38, p. 167). He read all that he could about Adams and reflected on his own experiences of and sentiments about his mentor. Everett organized the body of the speech according to Cicero's three topics: the blessings of fortune, the accomplishments of one's life, and the qualities of mind or character (1:243). He focused, as Adams himself had recommended, on the last: the unique qualities of Adams's character—those virtues that might be passed on for emulation by future generations. Everett would deliver an encomium, not a biography.

Everett presented his address at a day-long memorial in Boston's Faneuil Hall. Referred to by historian Lynn Parsons as *one of the first media events in American history* (Reid, 1990, p. 61), the event was covered by reporters from across the nation and attended by a delegation of dignitaries from every state in the Union. Everett did not disappoint his audience, expertly following his former teacher's advice to *mingle moral sentiment with oratorical splendor,* to *combine admirable sentiments with ardent panegyric,* and to *irradiate every gem of eloquence with a lucid beam of instruction* (10: p. 252).

Everett spoke for two hours and five minutes; the audience was packed so closely together that a reporter from the Salem Register observed that when one person moved the entire assemblage began *undulating like the ocean* (Papers, 38, p. 167). They listened in awed silence. With a modest acknowledgment of his lack of time to prepare, Everett announced that he would respect the wishes of those who invited him *to place on record a deliberate testimonial of your high sense of his [Adams's] exalted worth.*

Everett finds in the occasion, as he did in Worcester, an opportunity to declaim on the theme of Union. In his exordium, He evokes Adams's legacy as a man who honestly spoke his mind but never in anger and always with the larger goal of advancing the national interest. Indeed, Everett observes, it was precisely because Adams had abjured faction that each state had sent a delegation to the memorial service. And because of Adams's commitment to the *common good,* the Massachusetts legislature, itself composed of discordant opinions, had unanimously invited Everett to speak.

> *Falling, as he has done, at a period of high political excitement, and entertaining and expressing, as he ever did, opinions the most decided in the boldest and most uncompromising manner, he has yet been mourned, as an object of respect and veneration, by good men and patriots of every party name. Leaders, that rarely met him or each other but in opposition, unite in doing honor to his memory, and have walked side by side in the funeral train.*

Such circumstances, Everett infers, compel the eulogist to avoid rekindling any animosities that *time has long since subdued, and death has … extinguished forever.* Thus, says Everett in a poetic metaphor,

> *I come, at your request, to strew flowers upon the grave of an illustrious fellow-citizen, not to dig there, with hateful assiduity, for roots of bitterness.*

The occasion requires, in other words, that Everett engage in the appropriate moral approximations:

> *I shall aim to deprive my humble narrative of all the interest which it would derive from espousing present or past controversies. Some such I shall wholly pass over; to some I shall but allude; on none shall I dwell further than is necessary to acquit my duty…. But I am sure that I shall consult your feelings less than my own, if I try to follow our illustrious fellow-citizen through the various stages of his career, without mingling ourselves in the party struggles of the day; to exhibit him in the just lineaments and fair proportions of life, without the exaggerated colorings of passion; true to nature, but serene as the monumental marble; warm with the purest sympathies and deepest affections of humanity, but purified and elevated into the earthly transfiguration of genius, patriotism, and faith.*

Following a long narrative of Adams's life, Everett breaks free of the chains of biography in his arguments, and takes up the encomiast's charge: reviewing the qualities of Adams's character, his virtues.

Adams, Everett says, was a man of unimpeachable integrity who valued balance and proportion. In particular, Everett notes, Adams's congressional years were exemplary for the way in which he managed the slavery question, taking petitions from the many parties opposed to it and reading them into the Congressional Record even as he preserved his own neutrality. Adams's commitment to delicately balancing the competing interests he encountered made him the ultimate statesman. He rejoiced, for instance, in what Everett calls *that most illustrious act of Christian benevolence,* Great Britain's emancipating its slaves, and he eloquently advanced his constituents' case on the House floor. But he did so while assuring that, when the time to end slavery should come, he might serve as an honest broker among concerned parties. *His warmest opponents, while they condemned his policy,* Everett concludes, *admitted his sincerity, admired his courage, and owned his power.*

Everett continues his inventory of Adams's qualities of character. He was equally adept in all of his political dealings. In addition, he was a beloved teacher, a trusted advisor and friend to presidents, a scrupulous diplomat, and an utterly devoted public servant when he was himself the nation's chief executive. True it is, Everett acknowledges from behind the veil of silence that

> *As a man, he had, no doubt, the infirmities of human nature, (fair subjects of criticism to the happy few who are immaculate,) but not, I think, those most frequently laid to his charge.*

He was not, for instance, parsimonious or avaricious. He did not *load himself with debt,* as some had claimed. He was not inhospitable toward others while secretary of state, and he was plain in his personal habits, not flamboyant but *kind in nature* and *tender in feeling. A warmer spirit never dwelt in a human frame,* Everett concludes.

Having dispensed with the charges against Adams, Everett proceeds to enumerate the deceased president's positive qualities: he was a man who had a *lion heart* and a *religious spirit* (those two qualities Adams had urged on his students). Further, he was *a person of true courage, physical and moral.* He remained, even in life's darkest moments, a man of faith. Throughout his life, he inquired after truth. There was not a hint of affectation in the man, nor did he ever utter an unreflective opinion. In these ways, Everett concludes, did Adams reflect *the good old stock of which he came.*

The orator, having thus assayed his subject's virtues, was now ready to measure the man's life, to write, as it were, Adams's epitaph. Adams, Everett summarizes from the foregoing inventory of his virtues, was the embodiment of the essential qualities of character he had urged his students to seek in their own lives: living life to the fullest, but living it virtuously, in harmony and proportion as the times demanded. Therefore, Everett concludes,

> *The death of such a man is no subject of vulgar sorrow.*
> *Domestic affliction itself bows with resignation at an event*
> *so mature in its season; so rich in its consolations; so raised*
> *into sublimity by the grandeur of the parting scene. Of all*
> *the great orators and statesmen in the world, he alone has,*
> *I think, lived out the full term of a long life in actual ser-*
> *vice, and died on the field of duty, in the public eye, within*
> *the halls of public council. The great majority of public*
> *men, who most resemble him, drop away satisfied, perhaps*
> *disgusted, as years begin to wane; many break down at the*
> *meridian; in other times and countries, not a few laid their*
> *heads on the block. Demosthenes, at the age of sixty, swal-*
> *lowed poison, while the pursuer was knocking at the door*
> *of the temple in which he had taken refuge. Cicero, at the*
> *age of sixty-four, stretched out his neck from his litter to the*
> *hired assassin. Our illustrious fellow-citizen, in the fullness*
> *of his years and of his honors, upon a day that was shaking,*
> *in Europe, the pillars of monarchy to the dust, fell calmly at*
> *his post, amidst venerating associates, and breathed his last*
> *within the Capitol.*

> *And which is best and happiest yet, all this*
> *With God not parted from him,—*
> *But favoring and assisting to the end.*
> *Nothing is here for tears, nothing to wail,*
> *Or knock the breast; no weakness, no*
> *contempt, Dispraise of blame,—nothing but*
> *well and fair, And what may quiet us, in a*
> *death so noble.*

This is Adams's epitaph. He died happily, having achieved the Golden Mean: a full life lived virtuously. For those assembled, and for future generations such as ours, it could not have been put more beautifully.

The speech is presented in the mixed style Everett preferred for long orations. He uses a plain, conversational style when reviewing the long history of Adams's accomplishments. He is more emphatic in his language when refuting arguments about Adams's character. He then moves into the high oratory demanded of a memorable peroration. His choice of poetry to end the speech, his use of periodicity in the last sentence, his comparison of Adams to Demosthenes and Cicero— these aesthetic flourishes add erudition to the address, but exactly at that moment when they serve the purpose of driving home the point of the eulogy.

The speech is filled with elegant but appropriate figures. Note how the phrase,

> *to strew flowers upon the grave of an illustrious fellow-citizen, not to dig there, with hateful assiduity, for roots of bitterness,*

is evocative of nature, the realm to which Adams has now returned. A lucid figure adorns a thought, but it does more, it amplifies the thought itself.

The eulogy to John Quincy Adams exemplifies Adams's lecture on panegyric, as described in chapter 2. Everett applies every sentence of his beloved mentor's advice to that beloved mentor's eulogy. From the review of the three topics, to the focus on praise, to the moral approximations and *veils* due a man whose valor far exceeded any of his deficiencies or excesses in life, and finally to the pronouncement of the man's epitaph based upon the virtuousness of his life, Everett leaves Adams's *footprint in the sands of time,* to the utter satisfaction of those present and the nation at large.

Newspaper accounts of the speech were filled with praise. The Salem Register (April 20 1848) reported, for instance, that

> *The oration of Mr. Everett wanted nothing of his classic style, beauty of diction, and elegance of grace of oratory. If fatigue*

> *and disease had somewhat abated his energy in delivery, it*
> *had not rendered it less appropriate for a funeral discourse.*
> (Papers, 38, p. 167)

To which the Massachusetts' Barre Patriot (April 21, 1848) added,

> *The oration, when published, will add to the well earned*
> *fame of the orator, and be an undying tribute of respect to*
> *the name of Adams.* (Papers, 38, p.167)

THE CHARACTER OF WASHINGTON, 1856–60

Burnishing the *well earned fame of the orator,* Everett's remembrance
of Adams brought requests to deliver more eulogies. During the
ensuing years, Everett spoke at funerals and memorial addresses on
anniversaries or at dedications for personal friends, political allies,
famous, and not-so-famous dignitaries, even some from Europe,
whose lives had made an indelible mark on young America: Daniel
Webster, Abbott Lawrence; Thomas Dowse; Dr. Joseph Warren;
William Hickley Prescott; Henry Hallam; Alexander Von Humboldt;
Rufus Choate; Washington Irving; Lord Macaulay, Henry Gilpin,
Daniel Dewey Barnard; Nathan Appleton; Cornelius Conway Felton,
Nathan Hale, and Josiah Quincy. Through these orations, many
reprinted in pamphlet form and made available to the press and the
public, Everett became famous across the country. It was, then, a fate-
ful and fortuitous moment in his life when he encountered Miss Ann
Pamela Cunningham and George Washington's *weather-beaten* home
at Mount Vernon, both at once.

By 1855, Everett had settled peacefully back into retirement at his
home in Dorchester. It occurred to him that the coming year, 1856,
would mark the one hundredth anniversary of George Washington's
first visit to Boston, and he set out to write a speech on the man
who had significantly influenced his career as a politician and orator.
Around this time, Everett received an invitation to launch the 1855–56
lecture series sponsored by the Mercantile Library Association of
Boston. He declined at first; then he realized that the occasion would
give him an opportunity to celebrate Washington's visit and to debut

his lecture on the life and character of America's first president. Everett wrote to accept the invitation, asking that all proceeds from the speech be applied to some commemorative object to be placed in the library.

The speech, delivered on February 22, 1856, was an enormous success, and soon appeals to repeat it rolled in from across the country. Everett agreed to three performances, first in New Haven on February 27, then in New York on March 3 (where he stayed at the newly dedicated Everett House hotel), and then in Baltimore on March 11. The speech in New York was a resounding triumph, unparalleled in his career save perhaps for his Phi Beta Kappa Society oration of 1824. Delivered at the New York Music House, the speech drew a crowd of approximately six thousand people. As Everett wrote to a friend,

> *I never addressed—never saw assembled—such an audience. Every square inch of the vast opera house crowded: gentlemen and ladies standing in the aisles; the stage filled; and hundreds turned away who had tickets, owing to the fact that many went in without; for the door-keepers were overwhelmed. Once in, however, the attention was breathless and sustained to the last.* (Frothingham, p. 376)

The experience in New York buoyed Everett's spirits. En route to Baltimore, he stopped in Philadelphia where, in a fateful moment, friends introduced him to Miss Ann Pamela Cunningham, a founder of the Mount Vernon Ladies Association.[21] Cunningham, a crippled but dynamic woman, had struck out across the country to seek contributions to purchase, and eventually to restore, George Washington's home, which had fallen into a state of disrepair. She had heard Everett perform *Washington* in New York, and she understood that the orator could be of use to her cause. For his part, Everett was

---

21. Everett refers to this Association as the Ladies Mount Vernon Association. In other places it is noted as the Mount Vernon Association. The title used here is the present title, and the one for which the Association is best known.

touched by Cunningham's condition and by her resolve. The two pledged to work together to raise funds to buy Mount Vernon, at the time in the possession of John Augustine Washington III and tagged for sale at the price of two hundred thousand dollars.

Everett had received by this time an invitation to speak in Richmond for the benefit of *the Mount Vernon cause,* sponsored by the Ladies Association of Mount Vernon. The association was appealing to the Virginia legislature for funds to save the home. Everett refused at first, but then he accepted, dedicating the proceeds of the speech to the preservation of the storied property. The speech, given in Richmond on March 19, was another huge success, and it was quickly followed by similarly enthusiastic receptions in Petersburg, Charlottesville, Washington, Baltimore (again), Philadelphia, Princeton, Newark, Brooklyn, Providence, Charlestown, Springfield, Cambridgeport, Worcester, Salem, Hartford, and Taunton, all between March 21 and May 30. Considering Everett's age (sixty-two) and the difficulties of traveling in these early years of railroads and steam locomotion (it took four days to journey from Boston to Philadelphia, for instance), the first *run* of *The Character of Washington* was a tribute to the perseverance of Edward Everett as much as it was to the glory of George Washington.

After a February 23, 1857, anniversary delivery of *Washington* in Boston, Everett launched a nationwide tour that took him as far west as St. Louis and to many major cities in between, including Detroit, Chicago, Cincinnati, Lexington, Cleveland, and Buffalo. While on the road, he often spoke five nights a week, and at one point he traveled sixteen hundred miles in ten days. Even in moments of exhaustion, loneliness, noisy crowds, and bad food in poor hotels, Everett relished his status as a nineteenth-century superstar.

And as if these four years weren't larger than life already, it must be noted that at the same time he was doing *Washington,* Everett was also doing other orations on the lecturing circuits. For instance, he delivered his much sought after *Franklin, The Boston Boy,* twenty-eight times between January 1859 and February 1861. He often had overlapping engagements in cities such as New York, where he delivered *Washington* on March 4, *Franklin* on March 9, and

Washington again on March 11. It must be remembered that both of these speeches were lengthy orations; for instance, *Washington* generally extended between one hour and thirty minutes and one hour and forty minutes. Everett was proving himself to be an indefatigable speaker, dedicated to the goal he had set out for himself.

What was so compelling about this speech, *The Character of Washington*? Some such as Reid have suggested that the speech was actually a thinly veiled attempt to rally audiences to the cause of Union and thus avert the Civil War:

> *Everett recognized the persuasive value of the ceremonial address. Recollection of America's past glories, he had long believed, could serve to mitigate the hostilities of the present. Thrilled by 'Washington's' success and alarmed by sectionalist rift, Everett decided to employ the hero-symbol of Washington, beloved alike in North and South, in a rhetorical attempt to help save the Union.* (Reid, 1957, p. 145)

This understanding of the speech, while insightful from the perspective of ends or ulterior motives, would lead to the conclusion that it was at least partially a failure. But *The Character of Washington* was a rousing success, a speech that citizens of towns and cities across America clamored to hear. Just the fact that Everett raised $87,000 from his two tours of *Washington,* all of which went to saving Mount Vernon as a national monument, is enough to warrant its status as one of the most successful speeches of the nineteenth century. There is, indeed, another explanation for the enormous crowds and the adulation of the press for *The Character of Washington*: the speech is perfect for its times and the perfect embodiment of the times.

The Character of Washington is about *greatness.* As noted earlier, audiences loved to hear biographical lectures and, through them, discover how people had achieved greatness in their lives. Ralph Waldo Emerson's memorable 1841 essay *Self-Reliance,* much of which was rehearsed in his lyceum lectures, was in its essential character a speech about becoming great (it contained one of Emerson's most memorable epigrams: *To be great is to be misunderstood*). Frederick

Douglass's most popular lyceum lecture, *Self-Made Men,* was a tribute to men, black and white, who had achieved greatness through courage and hard work. Even Russell Conwell's legendary speech *Acres of Diamonds,* directed toward the acquisition of wealth, is best understood as a recipe for achieving greatness through personal inventiveness. Eulogies, too, were often used as vehicles for explaining to those assembled the qualities of character that produced greatness in the deceased.

So it was a natural for Everett to choose the theme of *greatness,* the very topic that not only exemplified his subject but that also compelled the interest of his audience. In the exordium of *Washington,* Everett moved directly to this central idea:

> *After briefly alluding to the three great eras in his life, in which he appeared before the people of the country in distinct and important characters, I shall offer you some views of the relation of Washington, not merely to the United States, but to the age in which he lived, and then endeavor to point out the true nature and foundation and distinctive character of his greatness. Grant me, I pray you, my friends, your candor, your indulgence, and your sympathy.*

But this speech would not be a eulogy; enough eulogies had been offered up for Washington, including his father's. No. This was to be a grand memorial—part lecture, part encomium, focused on the qualities of a man or woman's character, in this case Washington's, that comprised that individual's unique and defining source of greatness. In begging for the audience's indulgence, the great orator signals that he will need all of his powers of eloquence to portray for them not just that Washington was *great* but that he was *the greatest man of our own or of any age.* A difficult challenge, this, filled with the difficult choices orators must make as they survey the subject's virtues and arbitrate their subject's life for the audience. It is a challenge, however, that Everett enthusiastically accepts. Thus, just as he had done with Adams and dozens of times since, Everett sets out to measure Washington's life, guiding his audience to its essence.

Great men, great women, Everett begins his argument, rise
to notice in great times. Washington certainly did so, the orator
observes, for he was at the center of the three critical moments in the
birth of America. The first was the Seven Years War, about which
Everett had spoken at Worcester in 1833. Washington fought hero-
ically and survived while many others had died. Out of this turning
point in the struggle for independence, Washington earned a reputation for courage and upright conduct. His spirit was tried in the *fires
of disaster, and came out like thrice-refined gold.* Twenty-four years
old at the time, Washington was, as Everett describes him,

> *a model of manly strength and beauty, perfect in all the
> qualities and accomplishments of the gentleman and the
> soldier, but wise and thoughtful beyond his years, inspiring
> at the outset of his career that love and confidence which are
> usually earned only by a life of service.*

By 1776, Washington was already an American hero for whom
some heroic fate was clearly in store. Then, during the glorious
Revolution that resulted in America joining the family of nations,
again the figure of Washington looms over all others. How can it be
that in an age of heroes, Everett asks, Washington is the most heroic?
Everett is reluctant on this matter, but at the same time certain:

> *Heaven forbid that I should ascribe all the glory of this
> auspicious result to one man, even though that man were
> Washington: Heaven forbid that I should appear insensible
> to the merits of those by whom he was seconded and sustained,
> both in the revolutionary and constitutional age, of Franklin
> and Adams, of Henry and Jefferson, of Lafayette, of Green,
> of Knox and Lincoln, of Jay and Hamilton and Madison,
> men to whom the great chief himself never failed to do justice;
> but I say no more than each and all of these revered patriots
> would themselves have said, no more than several of them
> did say in pronouncing the character of Washington to have
> been the beacon light which guided the country through that*

broken and stormy sea. Beacon light did I say: it was more and higher. The tempest might rage, the ocean might heave from its depths, the eternal hills might tremble upon their rocky thrones, and the bewildered needle might wander from its path, but there was one:

As constant as the Northern Star,
Of whose true fixed and resting quality,
There is no fellow in the firmament.

And then, of course, the third period, Washington's selection to the Presidency, becomes a moment of national rejoicing. Everett captures the moment with a brilliant allusion to the toast made by Henry (Light Horse Harry) Lee,[22] on the floor of Congress upon his hearing of Washington's death in 1799:

Inured to military command from his youth, he sheathes his sword with all that gladness of heart with which unchastened ambition draws it: the first in war, he becomes (O, rare union of graces!!) the first in peace; and the first President of the United States was unanimously chosen in the hearts of the people.

In these three great times, then, are the qualities of Washington's character steeled. But other people have lived in momentous and challenging times. Were their characters not also equal to the occasion? Were they not also *great*? Appropriating one of his favorite rhetorical strategies, the comparison, Everett reviews a host of illustrious individuals: Frederick the Great; Catherine II; Alexander and Nicholas, the czars of Russia; King Charles XII of Sweden. More are named: the gifted statesman William Pitt, Captain Cook, General Wolfe, and even people who were called *great* such as Peter the Great.

---

22. Congressman Henry (Light Horse Harry) Lee: 'To the memory of the man, first in war, first in peace, and first in the hearts of his countrymen.' A resolution presented to the House of Representatives on the Death of George Washington, December 1799.

Even the scientists of the age, the thinkers, the explorers and adventurers, the inventors—all were to be considered. Everett discovers elements of greatness in each one of these world figures, but in some the greatness was borrowed or inherited, in some it was reflected from the deeds of others, and in some it was unoriginal. In even the best cases, the deeds of these others led to temporary triumphs and successes. For others, their greatness itself was but a temporary condition. For instance, Everett considers Napoleon, the man whose star looms brightest in the galaxy of greatness, whose career begins in triumph but ends in utter ruin, both for of himself and for of his country.

Proceeding as he does by example and comparison, Everett has structured the terms by which he will proceed to make his case for Washington.

> *Among all the wise in counsel, the valiant in battle, the firm and prudent in government, the pure in life, however eminent the single points of character, however meritorious their achievements, I find not one of any nation, in any part of this remarkable period of history, who has left so deep an impression of himself in the public opinion of mankind; not one, the sum total of whose qualities, and the aggregate of whose character, can be measured with that of our Washington.*

Washington's greatness is not inherited, it is not temporary, it is not compromised. What he achieved was not for himself but for others, and it has persisted; it is permanent. If Everett seeks to claim that Washington was the greatest man of any age, however, he must prove his hypothesis not simply by comparing Washington to the world's other supposedly *great* men and women, but by specifying the exact qualities of Washington's character that warrant this supremely distinctive title. *I am tasked to find an answer that does full justice to my own conceptions and feelings,* Everett notes. But, he suggests, he will try as best he can to convince his audience of the merits of his claim.

Everett's argument proceeds as follows. As great men proceed to act in great times, they become great because, in addition to putting their country's interests first, they bring to those times the exact virtues needed to triumph over the crises the times present. This is an ancient truth, Everett asserts, and so it is to the ancients that he turns to take proper measure of his subject.

> *The ancient philosophers placed the true conception of perfect manhood in the possession of those powers and qualities which are required for the honorable and successful discharge of the duties of life, each in the golden mean, equally removed from excess in either direction, and all in due proportion. This type of true greatness I find more fully realized in the character of Washington than in that of any other chieftain or ruler of ancient or modern times. He did not possess a few brilliant qualities in that exaggerated degree in which they are habitually ascribed to the heroes of poetry and romance; but he united all the qualities required for the honorable and successful conduct of the greatest affairs, each in the happy mean of a full maturity, and all in that true proportion in which they balance and sustain each other.*

Everett has now reached back again to his mentor's lecture 10, to Adams's recapitulation of Aristotle's list of virtues by means of which a man's life may be fairly assessed. These Everett will use to illustrate the qualities that suited Washington, more so than any individual in history to date, to the times in which he lived. And to describe those virtues, Everett echoes his father's eulogy to Washington offered five decades before.

Oliver Everett, who had also recounted Washington's role in the three momentous periods of America's founding, had lauded the general's qualities of piety, wisdom, perseverance, and courage during times of crisis. Edward, Oliver's son, revisits that list and then revises it: Washington's virtues are prudence, justice, modesty, and common sense. These are virtues of the mean, Everett reminds his audience, characteristics not often embodied in literature or praised by the public, but having the quality of moderation. When gathered together in one man, these virtues yield a balanced temperament capable of managing a crisis such as a revolution. Everett notes that *prudence,* for example, *receives no applause, excites no admiration, wins no love. Common Sense,* the orator continues,

> *takes no hold of the imagination; it inspires no enthusiasm, it wins no favor; it is well if it can stand its ground against the plausible absurdities, the hollow pretences, the stupendous impostures of the day.*

But when we look beyond the dazzle, Everett asserts, we find that Washington's virtues (prudence, modesty, justice, and common sense) characterize that *silent equilibrium of mental and moral power which governs the universe.*

Here is Everett's point. In times of danger and emergency—the Seven Years War, the Revolution, the Constitutional debates—when all could have been lost, America did not need an Alexander, a Caesar, a Napoleon, men who lived excessive lives, focused more on themselves than the larger cause. America needed a Washington to hold the ship of state steady, to *rebuke prosperous ambition,* to lead the nation with gentle firmness through the first chaotic hours of its birth. To complain that Washington was destitute of brilliance, Everett says,

> *is to complain of a circle that it has no salient points and no sharp angles in its circumference; forgetting that it owes all its wonderful properties to the unbroken curve of which every point is equidistant from the centre.*

To do so, the orator implies, would be absurd. It would be to miss the very beauty of the circle itself. Everett has chosen his words well. He has selected a metaphor his audience can picture: Washington is the greatest man of any age because he had exactly the right virtues for the historical moments in which he found himself. His appearance on history's stage was in perfect harmony with history's challenges. He embodies the Golden Mean. *No veil he needed,* Everett notes in a line of verse, *virtue proof, no thought infirm altered his cheek.* Not only is no veil of silence required but neither is the orator called upon to resort to moral approximation to define the greatness of Washington. His morality was pure, and, Everett concludes,

> *It is this which establishes its intimate relations with general humanity. On this basis he ceases to be the hero of America, and becomes the hero of mankind.*

In being brought to understand Washington's greatness, the audience can see a path by means of which they themselves might find greatness. Greatness is not the brashness of a Napoleon; it is not the shamelessness of monarchical opulence; it is not self-indulgence. Greatness is living according to the Golden Mean: nothing in excess, nothing in deficiency, and constantly striving to do the right thing at the right time for the right reason. Here is greatness that anyone can achieve. Few do and few will, but all can try. Inspirational, idealistic rhetoric, this, and in the age of the Greek revival an argument as appropriate, as perfectly situated, as Washington was in his time.

And from where do those virtues come? From Washington's Christian upbringing. Washington's virtues spring from a source common to all, or most, of those in the audience. Virtues such as modesty, prudence, justice, and common sense, are an essential part of the Brotherhood of Man as Everett had learned from Cicero, the divine attribute in the essence of each human being, given to them by God. If Washington could be great, so could every person in the audience. How uplifting!

Everett's peroration is a tribute to Washington right out of his father's eulogy. It is also the most *ardent* and *radiant* rhetoric of his career. We honor Washington, Everett asserts, when we live by the words of his Farewell Address: to abjure faction and preserve the Union at all costs. All that Everett had prophesied at Cambridge; all that he had urged at Worcester, Bunker Hill, Faneuil Hall, and across the nation—all was at stake now as the dogs of war were beginning to howl. The great promise of America, the land of unique possibilities, the City on a Hill—all were at risk. Everett exhorts Americans to *quit their ease,* as his father had said they would do, and raise their voices:

A great and venerated character like that of Washington,
which commands the respect of an entire population, how-
ever divided on other questions, is not an isolated fact
in history to be regarded with barren admiration, it is a
dispensation of Providence for good. It was well said by
Mr. Jefferson in 1792, writing to Washington to dissuade
him from declining a renomination: "North and South will
hang together while they have you to hang to." Washington
in the flesh is taken from us; we shall never behold him as
our fathers did; but his memory remains, and I say, let us
hang to his memory. Let us make a national festival and
holiday of his birthday; and ever, as the 22nd of February
returns, let us remember, that while with these solemn and
joyous rites of observance we celebrate the great anniversary,
our fellow-citizens on the Hudson, on the Potomac, from the
southern plains to the Western lakes, are engaged in the same
offices of gratitude and love. Nor we, nor they alone, beyond
the Ohio, beyond the Mississippi, along that stupendous trail
of immigration from east to west, which bursting into States
as it moves westward, is already threading the Western prai-
ries, swarming through the portals of the Rocky Mountains
and winding down their slopes, the name and the memory of
Washington on that gracious night will travel with the silver
queen of heaven through sixty degrees of longitude, nor part
company with her till she walks in her brightness through the
golden gate of California, and passes serenely on to hold mid-
night court with her Australian stars. There and there only,
in barbarous archipelagos, as yet untrodden by civilized man,
the name of Washington is unknown, and they, too, when
they swarm with enlightened millions, new honors shall be
paid with ours to his memory.

No one can fail to notice the grand and rousing oratory Everett
here employs. Martin Luther King Jr. would rally the nation a century
later with exactly the same populist appeal in his *I Have a Dream*
oration as he implored Americans from across the country to share

his vision of equal treatment for all. But although King's purpose has not been fully realized, Everett's was burst asunder over the issue of slavery, the matter Everett veils in the phrase *other questions*. By 1856, Everett knew that war was inevitable. Not even his rhetorical skills, Everett realized, honed as they were through a long and illustrious career in politics and international diplomacy, could stop it. As Lincoln would say in his second inaugural address,

> *Both parties deprecated war, but one of them would make war rather than let the nation survive, and the other would accept war rather than let it perish, and the war came.*

But even though the exhortation in *Washington* fell short of Everett's hopes, his audiences loved the oration, and he could have delivered it twice as often were the days available. *Washington* drew praise from across the nation by all those who heard it. One newspaper, the Indianapolis Journal, (May 6, 1857) printed this typical response after an Everett performance:

> *All pronounce the oration to be the finest tribute to the memory of Washington that has ever sounded in western ears. No words can describe it, and no criticism touch it.* (Reid, 1957, 151)

Not to be outdone, the Cincinnati Daily Enquirer wrote two days later that

> *For two hours he held his audience enchained by his clear, vigorous narrative, his vivid and graphic pictures, his pure and elevated reflections, his striking contrasts, his just, lucid, and philosophic views, all pervaded by a glowing earnestness and sincerity of feeling and warmth of patriotism which awoke a sympathetic thrill and response in every heart.* (Reid, 1957, p. 151)

Others who, as one reporter put it, *sat beneath the charmed flow of his eloquence,* described Everett's oration in words such as *enchanting* and *remarkable.* A St. Louis reporter commented:

> *It would be needless for us to speak of the graces of oratory, the ripe scholarship, or the finished rhetoric of one who has a national reputation in all these matters.* (Reid, 1957, p. 152)

The *Character of Washington* certainly *paid off* for the Mount Vernon Ladies Association. By the time he left the podium following his final presentation of *Washington* (in Lewiston, Maine, on April 24, 1860), Everett had sent approximately $87,000 dollars to the Mount Vernon Ladies Association. Even paying for his own travel and other expenses, Everett forwarded every penny of each evening's *Washington* lecture receipts to Miss Cunningham. Moreover, when he learned that the ladies needed ten thousand dollars to secure a loan for the purchase, he accepted a proposal from Robert Bonner, publisher of the widely circulated New York Ledger. Bonner offered to pay the $10,000 were Everett to agree to write a series of weekly articles on the life and times of George Washington. The essays, on such topics as Christmas customs, the financial crisis of 1857, lighthouses, Daniel Boone, and, of course, momentous events in Washington's life, were well received by the public and later published as the Mount Vernon Papers.

In 1857, following his first tour of *Washington,* by which time he had delivered the oration seventy times, Everett was honored by the Mount Vernon Ladies Association with a gold-headed cane that had belonged to the president. The presentation was made in a packed theatre in Richmond, the crowd overflowing into the city's streets. In his acceptance speech, Everett noted that, from his cradle, his life had been touched by the great hero. His first declamation in school had been about Washington:

> *From Vernon's mount behold the hero rise,*
> *Resplendent forms attend him to the skies.*

With characteristic modesty, Everett then accepted the cane.

> *For these efforts and the labor and time required by them, I claim no merit. I have asked, expected, no reward; least of all such a reward as I receive this day, sir, at your hands. It has truly been, as you have been pleased to say, a labor of love. I have felt that I was engaged in a pure and honorable work, tending directly to a noble end, and not unproductive, perhaps, of incidental good.*

Having now displayed his own character, Everett delivered *The Character of Washington* for the seventy-first time.

The Character of Washington deserves its place in history if for nothing more than its enormous success and its most notable outcome, the preservation of Washington's home as a national monument. A masterpiece of nineteenth-century elocution and perhaps the greatest exemplar of the Ciceronian oratory so loved by Americans during this period, it is a worthy study for any pupil of oratory. But like those rarest of orations such as Abraham Lincoln's *Gettysburg Address,* Elizabeth Cady Stanton's *The Solitude of Self,* or Martin Luther King Jr.'s *I Have a Dream, The Character of Washington* is also a composition both timely and timeless in its ideas and in its mastery of rhetorical techniques. Perhaps the Washington, D.C., Intelligencer put it best: *This great oration may be already considered as a part of the literature of the country* (Reid, 1957, p. 151).

THE ELOQUENCE OF EDWARD EVERETT: THE ROAD TO GETTYSBURG

Edward Everett was the pupil John Quincy Adams trained him to be. His oratory was perfectly adapted to the times. He was optimistic, idealistic, patriotic, conciliatory, and sentimental, as his era preferred. He was unique in his ability to combine eloquence and erudition. His integrity was unimpeachable. He remains the perfect exemplar of the Golden Age of American Oratory.

By 1863, as the Civil War raged into its third year and the fortunes of the North turned bleaker and bleaker, a battle of epic proportions was joined in Gettysburg, Pennsylvania, on July 1. It would continue for three bloody days, the result of which were more than fifty-four thousand soldiers dead, wounded, or missing but out of which came a turning point for the Union Army. As General George Herbert Meade surveyed the scene of carnage before him, he knew he could not chase General Robert E. Lee down the turnpike toward the Potomac River as aggressively as the situation demanded. Too many of his soldiers were lying wounded or dead and unburied in the fields and streams of Gettysburg. In addition, the people of the town of Gettysburg were in shock, having had their town briefly captured by Confederate soldiers and their land soaked with the blood of thousands of men, women, and animals. As Meade hesitated there, in the foothills of the South Mountains, a decision was being made by the governors of the states involved in the battle to create America's first national cemetery. An orator would be required to consecrate the site. In some not so small part because of *The Character of Washington,* the committee knew exactly who that man should be: Edward Everett. It would be Everett's most challenging oration but an occasion to which he would rise. On November 19, 1863, Edward Everett would present his Gettysburg Address. It is to this historic event that we now turn.

WORKS CITED

Adams, John Quincy. Lectures on Rhetoric and Oratory (1810). Reprint, Delmar, N.Y.: 1997.

Brewer, David J. The World's Best Orations. Ten Volumes. St. Louis and Chicago: Ferd P. Kaiser, 1899.

Everett, Edward. Papers. Massachusetts Historical Society. Vols. 146, 167, 249.

Everett, Oliver. Eulogy on General George Washington. Boston: Samuel Etheridge, 1800.

Frothingham, Paul Revere. Edward Everett: Orator and
    Statesman. Boston: Houghton Mifflin Company. 1925.

Grant, Michael, trans. Cicero: Selected Works. Baltimore:
    Penguin Books, 1967.

Murphy, James J., and Richard A. Katula. A Synoptic History of
    Classical Rhetoric. 3rd ed. Mahwah, N.J.: Lawrence
    Erlbaum Associates, 2003.

Reid, Ronald, *Edward Everett's, The Character of Washington,*
    Southern Speech Journal 22 (1957): 144–56.

Reid, Ronald. Edward Everett: Unionist Orator. New York:
    Greenwood Press, 1990.

Stebbins, Rufus, *Edward Everett as an Orator,* Cornell Era,
    January 12, 1872, pp. 195–98.

Edward Everett
at Gettysburg:
Sitting as Lincoln Speaks
November 19, 1863

4

The fittest man in the nation speaks at Gettysburg

> *Upon an issue in which the life of the country is involved,*
> *we rally as one man to its defence. All former differences of*
> *opinion are swept away; we forget that we have been parti-*
> *sans; we remember only that we are Americans, and that*
> *our country is in peril.*
> —*Edward Everett,* April 27, 1861

EDWARD EVERETT AND THE CIVIL WAR

The Civil War came suddenly. It had for years seemed inevitable to individuals such as Edward Everett; nevertheless, when Southern guns fired on Fort Sumter on April 12, 1861, the North was as stunned as it was unprepared. For years the North had rationalized that threats of secession were little more than, as William Lloyd Garrison had taunted, the *barkings of a dog that would not bite* (Frothingham, p. 417). And so, when Abraham Lincoln, the new and untested president who had won a bitterly contested election, called for the nation to supply troops on April 15th, the move came as a rude awakening.

Edward Everett had half-heartedly accepted the vice-presidential nomination of the Constitutional Union Party for the 1860 election. His running mate was John Bell of Tennessee, one of many Southern conservatives who hoped, like Everett, that despite all signs to the contrary, the Union could be saved if the slavery question were left out of the campaign. Bell and Everett, who had been friends in Congress, now found themselves thrown together in a futile attempt to rally Americans to the cause of preserving the Union. Neither was energized by the prospects, and when the votes were tallied, they had finished last in the popular vote and third out of four parties in the electoral vote. Despite their final position in the balloting, it is quite likely that the team of Bell and Everett was responsible in part for Lincoln's nomination at the 1860 Republican Party Convention. This was so because it had been determined that William Seward, favored for the nomination, could not hold the upper South, as could Lincoln, against a Bell-Everett ticket (Donald, p. 247).

The Republican Party's platform had proclaimed that slavery should be excluded from the new Nebraska territories, and the South read Lincoln's election as the end of any further debate on the question. In the North, too, Lincoln's victory was interpreted, as Frothingham puts it, that *There was to be no more temporizing, no further attempts at compromise. Slavery was an evil, and it should not be extended* (p. 413).

Although this idea was implied in Lincoln's election, the new president never actually made such a statement; rather, he remained essentially silent on the matter of slavery during the interim period between the November election and his inauguration in March 1861. (Donald, pp. 259–260) His commitment to holding the Union together, however, was absolute. Like so many, including Edward Everett, Lincoln believed that, as David Donald puts it, *Unionists were in a large majority throughout the South and that, given time for tempers to cool, they would be able to defeat the secessionist conspirators* (p. 260). Lincoln did not care how this happened; only that it did. In his inaugural address on March 4, Lincoln practically begged for peace between the two sides. *I am loth [sic] to close,* the president declared,

> *we are not enemies, but friends. We must not be enemies....*
> *the mystic chords of memory, stretching from every battlefield,*
> *and patriot grave, to every living heart and hearthstone, all*
> *over this broad land, will yet swell the chorus of the Union,*
> *when again touched, as surely they will be, by the better*
> *angels of our nature.*

Lincoln's message was George Washington's; it was Oliver Everett's; it was Edward Everett's. Everett had dedicated his entire oratorical career to preserving the Union. Now, despite the president's poetic appeal, he watched the nation plunge into chaos. Just as they had dealt poorly with abolitionists over the past thirty years, Everett observed, Washington politicians had no realistic strategy for dealing with the secessionists. It was clear to him that war was on the horizon, but he understood it to be not the demise of his four-decade crusade to save the Union but an interlude brought on by radicals from both the North and the South (Frothingham, p. 413). He saw the Civil War as a lesson to the nation that the independence it had won at such peril was a blessing worth fighting to preserve. He also recognized that this was war, that it must be won at any cost, and that he must now take sides. He did so by immediately throwing his full support behind Abraham Lincoln, a man who shared his commitment to Union, and by vowing to do whatever he could to help put down the insurrection and reunite the nation.

Everett's decision was resolute. *Disapproving as I did conscientiously of the course of policy pursued by the Republican Party,* he wrote, *I disapprove much more of the Secessionists* (Varg, p. 200). His elated brother-in-law, Charles Francis Adams, wrote that Everett's interests now *ran on all fours with his convictions* (Varg, p. 200). Adams would later comment, *To me, his last four years appear worth more than all the rest of his life, including the whole series of his rhetorical triumphs* (Varg, p. 200). On April 18, six days after the first shots had been fired, Everett accepted a request to speak about the war effort in Boston's Chester Square. His words were clear. Turning to the American flag waving in the breeze, and in his now familiar and most forceful patriotic tones, Everett said,

All hail to the flag of the Union! Courage to the heart
and strength to the hand to which in all times it shall be
entrusted! May it ever wave in unsullied honor over the
dome of the Capitol, from the country's strongholds, on
the tented field, upon the wave rocked top-mast. It was
originally displayed on the 1st of January, 1776, from the
head-quarters of Washington, whose lines of circumvallation
around beleaguered Boston traversed the fair spot where we
now stand; and as it was first given to the breeze within the
limits of our beloved State, so may the last spot where it shall
cease to float, in honor and triumph, be the soil of our own
Massachusetts. (Orations, 1895, 4:329)

EVERETT'S FAME AS AN ORATOR

By 1860, Edward Everett had become the most famous orator in
America. He had spent the previous four years presenting *The*
Character of Washington across the nation. In addition to *Washington,*
Everett had continued his work eulogizing departed notables; dedicating libraries, asylums, and schools; and presenting after-dinner
speeches on a wide variety of topics. Two of his speeches, *Franklin,*
The Boston Boy and *Charitable Institutions and Charity,* earned
national prominence and were repeated on numerous occasions, the
latter earning, by Everett's accounting, approximately $13,500 *for*
the benefit of various charitable institutions (Reid, 1990, p. 85). By
1858, Everett was one of only a handful of Northern Americans still
welcome and sought out for speaking engagements in the American
South—mostly the upper South. Once the war began, however, he
broke with his Southern acquaintances, even his dear friend Miss
Ann Pamela Cunningham, the woman with whom he had so success-
fully collaborated for the previous four years to save Mount Vernon
(Frothingham, pp. 421–22).

Once Everett publicly declared himself on the war, the North
embraced him, and he was invited repeatedly to speak throughout
the Union states. He accepted as many engagements as he could
squeeze into his calendar. His earliest and most notable address, *The*

Question of the Day, was presented to an enormous audience in New York City's Academy of Music auditorium on the 4th of July, 1861. The burden of his argument was Lincoln's: that the seceding states had committed treason, that they had broken the inviolable contract forged in the ratification of the Constitution. The South had agreed to form *a more perfect Union,* Everett asserted, but now it was applying the twisted logic that because it had the right to make the contract, it had the right to break it. Everett ridiculed this interpretation: *to deduce from the sovereignty of the States the right of seceding from the Union is the most stupendous non sequitur that was ever advanced in grave affairs* (Orations, 1895, 4:363). His peroration that evening was as patriotic, and yet as conciliatory, as any he had ever presented, and it was eerily reminiscent of his father's peroration in his eulogy on George Washington:

> *We wage no war of conquest and subjugation; we aim at nothing but to protect our loyal fellow-citizens, who, against fearful odds, are fighting the battles of the Union in the disaffected States, and to reestablish, not for ourselves alone, but for our deluded fellow-citizens, the mild sway of the Constitution and the Laws. The result cannot be doubted. Twenty millions of freemen, forgetting their divisions, are rallying as one man in support of the righteous cause—their willing hearts and their strong hands, their fortunes, and their lives, are laid upon the altar of the country. We contend for the great inheritance of constitutional freedom trans- mitted from our revolutionary fathers. We engage in that struggle forced upon us, with sorrow, as against our mis- guided brethren, but with high heart and faith, as we war for that Union which our sainted Washington commended to our dearest affections. The sympathy of the civilized world is on our side, and will join us in prayers to Heaven for the success of our arms.* (Orations, 1895, 4:405–6)

The speech in New York City was an immediate success, and it was quickly turned into a pamphlet to be distributed throughout the country and in Europe. Everett was now hounded to speak—*worked like a drayhorse*—as he put it (Frothingham, p. 425). He began composing a lecture entitled *The Causes and Conduct of the War.*

On October 16, 1861, upon its invitation, Everett delivered *The Causes and Conduct of the War* to the Mercantile Library Association of Boston. The speech was like a war rally, and it received a rousing welcome from the audience. Everett went on to deliver the speech fifty-eight more times, across the Northern states from Massachusetts to Iowa, concluding in Dubuque on June 20, 1862 (Orations, 1895, 4:490). Reid argues that it was Everett's credibility as a man of moderation and conciliation that was so appealing to audiences who went to hear his *Causes and Conduct* lecture (1990, p. 91). As Reid reminds us, in the northern United States, the Civil War was not a dispute between those who favored slavery and those who did not but among Americans whose views ran the spectrum from complete indifference to radical abolitionism (1990, p. 94). Everett had no position on the matter other than declaring slavery to be an evil that he believed Divine Providence would end in its own appointed time. But now, as he dedicated himself to winning this war of secession, Everett possessed credibility as a man of moderation and conciliation. In short, he was especially persuasive to *waverers,* as Horace Greeley called them in his article praising Everett's speech (Reid, 1990, pp. 91, 94).

At the same time, Everett's arguments in *Causes and Conduct* are noteworthy for their development of his thought. Not only do they presage both his and, to a lesser extent, Lincoln's Gettysburg addresses, but in the lecture Everett lifts the veil he had hitherto imposed on himself on the divisive issue of slavery. He argues that radicals in the South had been preparing to secede for decades prior to 1860, disputing, for example, what they called the unfair cotton tariffs inflicted by the United States Congress. Everett is loath to discuss slavery, he notes, because it was a pretext, not a cause, of secession. Radicals in the South, he asserts, were dissatisfied with forty years of compromise on the issue of slavery because *her leaders were predetermined not to be satisfied* (Orations, 1895, 4:473). The 1808 prohibition of the African slave trade written into the Constitution—the document even Southern leaders had ratified—all assumed, would lead to slavery's demise. But now Southerners were raising the issue simply because, pursuing their own selfish interests, they wanted out of the Union. Everett was, in the opinion of most historians, wrong about this assertion, but it was his conviction and he argued it forcefully.

Everett also issues a warning about the Southern secession, arguing that should it be successful, more areas of the country will feel free to withdraw from contracts made, more governments will spring up requiring more armies, more treaties, and more boundaries, and the inevitable friction among them will, as it has in Europe for centuries, lead to wars. As states divide into smaller entities, the once unique system of government established by the Founders will split into pieces, *and this great prosperous Union,* Everett predicts, *like the German Empire in the Middle Ages, will be broken up into hundreds of contemptible principalities* (Orations, 1895, 4:484). The Union, Everett hoped, was not to become a *rope of sand*; it would be restored, he believed, by the will of the citizenry in memory of the Revolutionary struggle that produced the greatest form of government ever known to mankind.

Everett's peroration in *Causes and Conduct* is familiarly Christian and patriotic, a reprise in his own words of his father Oliver's peroration in his eulogy to Washington from the man who had now become patriotism's voice.

> *This glorious national fabric shall not be allowed to crumble into dishonorable fragments. This seamless garment of union, which enfolds the States like a holy Providence, shall not be permitted to be torn in tatters by traitorous hands. No, a thousand times no! Rise, loyal millions of the country! Hasten to the defense of the menaced Union! Come, old men and children! Come, young men and maidens! Come with your strong hands; come with your cunning hands; come with your swords; come with your knitting needles; come with your purses, your voices, your pens, your types, your prayer; come one, come all, to the rescue of the country!*
> (Orations, 1895, 4:489)

Beyond Everett's reputation as a man of moderation, the success of *Causes and Conduct* is due, in part, to his rhetoric. He is a famous wordsmith, and this talent is clearly on display in motivational and pathos-filled passages such as the one above. His arguments made sense, especially to those many moderate citizens who now saw no other way to address slavery except through war. His peroration, which wrapped the American flag around the war effort, was an image aimed at the heart, one that roused the audience's patriotism. Little wonder it is that *Causes and Conduct* raised large sums of money for the Union's struggle. Everett was praised across the nation. Paul Varg reports that *After hearing the speech in Brooklyn, Henry Ward Beecher came to Everett and said excitedly that the address made him feel like enlisting* (p. 202).

EVERETT AT GETTYSBURG

Everett's renown was enhanced by his patriotic effort in *Causes and Conduct.* He had now saved Mount Vernon and rallied the nation to support the troops. When war came to the small town of Gettysburg, Pennsylvania on July 1, 1863, Everett was the most respected and influential orator in America. It was no surprise, then, that when the governors of the Union states met and appointed local townsman David Wills to supervise the construction of a national cemetery and to engage in a fitting memorial service to those Union soldiers who had died in battle during the three bloody days at Gettysburg, the executives unanimously agreed that Edward Everett should deliver the event's main oration. In their deliberations, they noted that

> *The consecration of the Cemetery Grounds was in due time suggested by Governor Curtin. The name of Edward Everett was submitted to the governors of all the states interested, as the Orator to deliver the address on that occasion, and they unanimously concurred in him as the person eminently suitable for the purpose. His great reputation as a scholar and an Orator, and his acknowledged and unselfish patriotism, and his years of toil to rescue the grove of Washington from*

neglect and decay, and make it the common property of the
Union, rendered him the fittest man in the nation for the
occasion. (Papers, 46, p. 233)

The invitation was sent to Everett on September 23, 1863. He
responded immediately, understanding this to be his most glorious
moment on the public stage. In his letter to the governors, Everett
accepted with humility and asked that the date be set for November 19.

I have received your favor of the 23rd, inviting me on behalf
of the governor's [sic] of the states interested in the prepara-
tion of a cemetery for the soldiers who fell in the great battles
of July last, to deliver an address at the consecration. I feel
much complimented by this request and would cheerfully
undertake the performance of a duty at once so interesting
and honorable. It is, however, wholly out of my power to
make the requisite preparations by the 23rd of October. I
am under engagements which will occupy all my time from
Monday next to the 12th of October, and indeed it is doubtful
whether, during the whole month of October, I shall have a
day at my command.

The occasion is one of great importance, not to be dismissed
with a few sentimental or patriotic commonplaces. It will
demand as full a narrative of the events of the three impor-
tant days, as the limits of the hour will admit, and some
appropriate discussion of the political character of the great
struggle of which the battle of Gettysburg is one of the most
momentous incidents. As it will take me two days to reach
Gettysburg, and will be highly desirable that I should at
least have one day to survey the battle field, I cannot safely
name an earlier time than the 19th of November. Should
such a postponement of the day first proposed be admis-
sible, it will give me great pleasure to accept the invitation.
(Papers, 46, p. 233)

Wills accepted the request, immediately responding to Everett that the date was fixed as November 19. Everett began his research, a diligent review of published papers, correspondence with those who were in the battle, and eyewitness accounts that he gleaned from newspapers. He comments on his exhaustive effort as follows.

> *Besides the sources of information mentioned in the text, I have been kindly favored with a memorandum of the operations of the three days drawn up for me by direction of Major General Meade (anticipating the promulgation of his official report) by one of his aides, Colonel Theodore Lyman, from whom I also have received other important communications relative to the campaign. I have received very valuable documents relative to the battle from Major General Halleck, Commander-in-Chief of the Army, and have been much assisted in drawing up the sketch of the campaign by detailed reports, kindly transmitted to me in manuscript from the Adjutant General's office, of the movements of every corps of the Army, for each day, after the breaking up from Fredericksburg commenced. I have derived much assistance from Colonel John B. Bachelder's oral explanations of his beautiful and minute drawing (about to be engraved) of the field of the three days' struggle. With the information derived from these sources I have compared the statements of General Lee's official report of the campaign, dated 31st July, 1863, a well-written article, purporting to be an account of the three days' battle, in the Richmond Enquirer of the 22nd of July, and the article on "The Battle of Gettysburg and the Campaign of Pennsylvania," by an officer, apparently a colonel in the British Army, in Blackwood's Magazine for September."* (Wills, pp. 49–50)

Everett completed the address while at home, committed it to memory, sent a copy to Lincoln, had the speech set in type by the Boston Daily Advertiser, pasted a copy of it into a small binder, and set off for Gettysburg on November 16 (Freidel, p. 2). Two days later, he arrived in Gettysburg, where he was met by David Wills and escorted to his room at Wills's home. He was not able to tour the battlefields due to high winds and threatening weather, and so, as he wrote, *I passed the morning in my chamber, gathering up my focus for tomorrow* (Papers, Vol 40, p. 182). Everett took tea with Professor Thaddeus Stevens of Gettysburg College during the afternoon, and then at 5:00 P.M., he went to the train station with Wills to meet Lincoln. Wills held a dinner in the president's honor, which Everett attended. In the evening, Everett retired to his room to practice his speech and prepare for the following day.

The next morning, Everett traveled to the cemetery in a carriage with Dr. T. H. Stockton, president of Gettysburg College. Upon reaching the grounds, Everett inspected the tent behind the platform, which he had requested for the purpose of relieving himself during the day's events. He was not happy with it. Nevertheless, Lincoln's party arrived and the ceremonies began with a long prayer and then a funeral dirge by Benjamin French. Everett, seated to the right of the president, was introduced. He rose and proceeded to deliver his Gettysburg Address. He reflected in his diary that

> *I omitted a good deal of what I had written, but was never-*
> *theless 2 hours long. Parts of the address were poorly memo-*
> *rized, several long paragraphs condensed, several thoughts*
> *occurred at the moment as happens generally. The great*
> *multitude assembled, many of whom had been standing four*
> *hours, listened without apparent weariness. After I had done,*
> *the President pressed my hand with great fervor and said "I*
> *am more than gratified, I am grateful to you."*
> (Papers, 40, p. 182)

After he returned to his seat, the program continued with a dirge written by Benjamin French. Everett may have excused himself to use the facilities prepared for him behind the stage, and it is unclear whether he returned in time to hear the president's brief *Dedicatory Remarks*. He made no comment in his diary about what has come to be known as Lincoln's *Gettysburg Address*. Nevertheless, one day later, as he reflected on the speech, Everett wrote to the president, saying among other things that *I should be glad if I could flatter myself that I came as near to the central idea of the occasion, in two hours, as you did in two minutes* (Frothingham, p. 458). This line is one of the most oft-quoted responses to Lincoln's address. It is less well known that Lincoln, in his turn, wrote to Everett voicing equal praise and admiration:

> *Your kind note of today is received. In our separate parts yesterday you could not have been excused to make a short speech, not I a long one. I am pleased to know that, in your judgment, the little I did say was not entirely a failure. Of course, I knew Mr. Everett would not fail; and yet, while the whole discourse was eminently satisfactory, and will be of great value, there were passages in it which transcended my expectations.* (Frothingham, p. 458)

Reactions to a speech often tell us much about it, but reactions to Everett's address do not, for they are as varied as the writers' or the observers' points of view. Lincoln was obviously pleased. Benjamin French, author of the hymn played during the ceremony, said that *it could not be surpassed by mortal man* (Goodwin, p. 585). French also observed that Everett *left his audience in tears many times during his masterly effort* (Donald, p. 464). Some reports indicate that near the end of the address a few in attendance began to wander the battlefields, but there is also testimony that the audience remained attentive throughout the address. That evening, Professor Stevens called on Everett to express his thanks for the speech. Everett apologized for *the inadequacy and possible errors of my sketch of the battles,* but Stevens praised the effort and said it was *not only correct, but executed with skill and tact* (Papers, 40, p. 182). Other citizens wrote to Everett about the narrative portion of the address, one concerned that he had not spent enough time praising General Joshua Reynolds, and another saluting Everett for raising Gettysburg *into permanent and historical importance*

(Papers, 32, p. 118). Perhaps the most romantic observation came from a reporter, John Russell Young, who was awed as much by the mere presence of Everett as by his speech:

> *His antique, courtly ways, fine keen eyes, the voice of singular charm ... the soft white hair, sunny, silken, clinging.... He seemed like some stately comrade of Adams and Jay stepped out from the sacred past.... He spoke without notes. Now and then he would take a sip of water. His voice was clear, satisfying, every note in tune, no sign of age.... A marvelous memory heard with the deepest attention.... Little applause ... no invitation to applause. I felt as I looked at the orator as if he was some antique Greek statue, so ... beautiful ... but so cold.* (Freidel, p. 2)

One week later, David Wills wrote to Everett requesting a copy of the address, which was to be published and used as a recruiting tool. Everett, of course, agreed, noting that *the proceeds of the publication shall be appropriated to the fund for the erection of a monument to the brave men whose remains are deposited in the cemetery* (Papers, 40, p. 182).

Press accounts of the address are inconsistent with one another and seem to run along party or sectional lines; whether critical or commendatory, however, the address received extensive treatment. Reid reports, for instance, that twenty-five metropolitan Republican-leaning daily newspapers took note of the speech, with twenty-one reproducing the entire text or portions of it. Eighteen anti-administration big-city newspapers also critiqued the address, eleven of them reproducing the text or a section thereof. One hundred seven weekly or small town papers covered the address, many quoting segments of the address on the front page. The speech was also widely mentioned in magazines, thus assuring a wide readership beyond Gettysburg (Reid, 1990, p. 100).

Many newspaper editorials in the North were filled with praise for Everett's address. The Boston Journal complimented the address for its accuracy:

> *The detailed narrative of the campaign ending in the battle*
> *of Gettysburg reads like the most brilliant pages of Macaulay*
> *or Prescott.... It is probably the best history of the campaign*
> *which this generation shall have the privilege of reading.*
> (Wills, p. 51)

Other commentaries suggest that expectations were not met. For instance, the editor of the Philadelphia Age wrote that

> *Seldom has a man talked so long and said so little. He gave*
> *us plenty of words, but no heart. He talked like a historian*
> *or an encyclopedist, or an essayist, but not like an orator.*
> (Goodwin, p. 585)

The Washington, D.C., Evening Union of December 5, also characterized the speech as *cold as an icicle.* The Harrisburg, Pennsylvania, Weekly Patriot and Union (November 26) printed a letter in which the writer, clearly an antiwar advocate, says

> *We can readily conceive that the thousands who went there*
> *as mourners, in view of the burial place of their dead, to*
> *consecrate, so far as human agency could, the ground in*
> *which the slain heroes of the nation, standing in the relation-*
> *ship to them of fathers, husbands, brothers, or connected by*
> *even remoter ties of marriage or consanguinity, were to be*
> *interred. To them the occasion was solemn; with them the*
> *motive was honest, earnest, and honorable. But how was it*
> *with the chief actors in the pageant, who had no dead buried*
> *or to be buried there; from none of those loins had sprung a*
> *solitary hero, living or dead, of this war which was begot-*
> *ten by their fanaticism and has been ruled by their whims.*
> *They stood there, upon that bloody ground, not with hearts*
> *stricken with grief or elated by ideas of true glory, but coldly*
> *calculating the political advantages which might be derived*
> *from the solemn ceremonies of the dedication.*

The writer then excuses Edward Everett, but only partially.

> *We will not include in this category of heartless men the*
> *orator of the day; but evidently he was paralyzed by the*
> *knowledge that he was surrounded by unfeeling, mercenary*
> *men, ready to sacrifice their country and the liberties of*
> *their countrymen for the base purpose of retaining power*
> *and accompanying wealth. His oration was therefore cold,*
> *insipid, unworthy of the occasion and the man.* (p. 3)

As the Amherst, New Hampshire, Farmer's Cabinet (November 26) summarized, *The address of Mr. Everett at Gettysburg is very lengthy, and eloquent, but does not seem to come up to the point of expectation.*

Southern newspapers mocked the speech. Typical was a report from the Macon, Georgia, Daily Telegraph, (December 3) in which Everett is accused of *astonishing and unaccountable* logic in his argument against states rights.

> *... when a political scholar (but no politician) like Everett*
> *talks of States Rights as a "wretched absurdity" we see in the*
> *future, for whoever may be its victims that most intolerable*
> *of despotisms—the despotism of an aggregate and irrespon-*
> *sible majority—a despotism which must grind until it pro-*
> *duces a real civil war—anarchy, and finally finds its relief in*
> *a military autocracy.* (p. 1)

Later commentary on the speech is also mixed. In 1890, in their book Abraham Lincoln: A History, Lincoln's aids John Nicolay and John Hay praised the speech for its historical accuracy and its gravity, which they deemed perfect for the occasion.

> *Edward Everett made an address worthy alike of his fame*
> *and the extraordinary occasion.... It is not too much to say*
> *that for the space of two hours he held his listeners spellbound*
> *by the rare power of his art.... If there was an American*

> *who was qualified by moral training, by literary culture, by*
> *political study, by official experience, and ripe experience in*
> *public utterance, to sit in calm judicial inquiry on the causes,*
> *theories, and possible results of the civil war, that man was*
> *Edward Everett. [His speech] embodies the calm reflection of*
> *the thinker in his study, pronounced with the grave authority*
> *of the statesman on his tribune.* (quoted in Wills, p. 51)

Some critics appreciated, while others did not, Everett's extended
account of the three days of battle. Some critics agreed, while others did not, with Everett's arguments about the cause of the war.
Garry Wills asserts that, while the speech was the *crowning effort* of
Everett's career, it failed because it looked backward while Lincoln's
speech looked forward (Wills, p. 52). Historians such as David
Donald and Doris Kearns Goodwin for their part have determined
that the address was satisfactory, but not much more (Donald, p. 464;
Goodwin, p. 585).

The wide-ranging, sometimes contradictory reactions, both short-
term and long-term, lead inexorably to a closer look at the speech
itself, particularly the historical account of the battles and the arguments made against the secession.

From a rhetorical point of view, the address is divided into the
classic parts of an oration, as follows: exordium, paragraphs 1–4; statement of the controversy, paragraph 5; narration, paragraphs 6–38;
arguments, paragraphs 39–47; peroration, paragraphs 48–58.[23]

The exordium is intended, through imagery, to set the scene and
the mood of the event:

> *Standing beneath this serene sky, overlooking these broad*
> *fields now reposing from the labors of the waning year, the*
> *mighty Alleghenies dimly towering before us, the graves*

---

23. The speech with paragraphs numbered is available at
www.AmericanLyceum.neu.edu. Use the Readings link and then
click on Edward Everett manuscripts to access the electronic file.

of our brethren beneath our feet, it is with hesitation that
I raise my poor voice to break the eloquent silence of God
and nature. But the duty to which you have called me
must be performed; grant me, I pray you, your indulgence
and your sympathy.

The orator then references the precedent for such funeral orations in the ancient Greek custom of the epitaphios logos, or eulogy, particularly the eulogy pronounced by Pericles to honor the soldiers who had died during the first year of the Peloponnesian War in 430 bce. Everett proclaims that he must do no less to honor those who died at Gettysburg, thus elevating the war to save the American Union to a status equivalent with the war to save the Athenian democracy. Not to commemorate the event, he avers, *to prove insensible to every prompting of patriotic duty and affection,* would be shameful:

> *... not only would you, fellow citizens, gathered, many of*
> *you from distant states, who have come to take part in these*
> *pious offices of gratitude—you, respected fathers, brethren,*
> *matrons, sisters, who surround me—cry out for shame, but*
> *the forms of brave and patriotic men who fill these honored*
> *graves would heave with indignation beneath the sod.*

Even though the remainder of Everett's speech would not follow the pattern of Pericles' Funeral Oration as Lincoln's speech did, both Pericles and Everett understood the need for rousing oratory to steel the resolve of those engaged in a momentous struggle to save their nation. Also, since the Greek Revival movement continued to form the cultural subtext of American life in 1863, the comparison with Pericles would have been familiar and appropriate.

The statement of controversy is concise and beautifully phrased using his customary technique of periodic sentences:

> *We have assembled, friends, fellow citizens, at the invitation*
> *of the Executive of the great central state of Pennsylvania,*
> *seconded by the Governors of seventeen other loyal states of*

the Union, to pay the last tribute of respect to the brave men, who, in the hard fought battles of the first, second, and third days of July last, laid down their lives for the country on these hill sides and the plains before us, and whose remains have been gathered into the Cemetery which we consecrate this day. As my eye ranges over the fields whose sods were so lately moistened by the blood of gallant and loyal men, I feel, as never before, how truly it was said of old, that it is sweet and becoming to die for one's country.

Everett now proceeds to his long narrative of the struggle against Southern aggression, and since accuracy is an important consideration for an orator taking on the role of historian, Everett's speech should be evaluated in that regard. He wrote himself of the difficulty he faced:

The close observation, which I have had occasion to make of the accounts of Meade's Campaign in July have convinced me, more than I ever felt it before, how uncertain the accounts of the great battles must be. By dexterous selection of details and choice of words, the very same incidents are related in a directly opposite manner by the two parties. (Freidel, p. 2)

Although later accounts, such as the one written by Frederick Tilberg and published by the National Park Service in 1962, would provide more and different details, Everett's are remarkably accurate given the limitations of the early accounts of the battles he had available to him. Everett's description of Pickett's Charge, for instance, that momentous battle of the third day that turned the tide for the Union, although not as rich in detail, is close to that provided by the National Park Service, especially in the important area of casualties named. Furthermore, Everett's tally of the numbers of lost, wounded, or missing soldiers on both sides squares quite well with official data that has been accumulated in the years since the close of the war.

There were minor gaffes. For example, Lincoln listened intently to

Everett's chronology, noting at one point to Seward that Everett had said *General Lee* when he meant *General Meade*. And if there were a major error, it was in Everett's account of Meade's efforts to overtake Lee and destroy his badly wounded army. Meade's venture was half hearted at best: only one brigade, under the command of General Governeur K. Warren, chased the Southern general, Richard S. Ewell, down toward the Potomac. Everett had relied on reports by one of Meade's aides, Colonel Theodore Lyman, and in doing so left himself open to bias.

Overall, however, Everett cannot be faulted for the errors of others. He took the accounts presented to him as having been made in good faith. Historian Irving Bartlett's appraisal of Everett's attempt to recount the battles of Gettysburg is concise:

> *The people got what they wanted from Everett—a long, erudite discourse connecting the valor and sacrifice demonstrated on that American battlefield with the heroic struggles toward freedom in the classical and modern world. He not only justified the Union cause with arguments in a manner Webster would have admired, but he demonstrated a masterly understanding of the battle's details drawn from journalistic accounts and the reports of Union officers.* (Bartlett, p. 460)

David Donald's assessment is likewise succinct: *For the most part it was a clear exposition ... of just what had happened during those fiercely hot three days in July when the nation's life hung in the balance* (p. 464).

If there is a problem with Everett's history, it is in the remarks that conclude this part of his speech. Although they are understandable from an orator's perspective, charged as he is with avoiding invective and emphasizing the good, from a historian's perspective—that is, the one Everett announced he was taking—they stray into a romanticism that transgresses the boundaries of objectivity as is evident in the following excerpt:

These were the expiring agonies of the three days' conflict, and with them the battle ceased. It was fought by the Union army with courage and skill, from the first cavalry skirmish on Wednesday morning to the fearful rout of the enemy on Friday afternoon, by every arm and every rank of service, by officers and men, by cavalry, artillery, and infantry. The superiority of numbers was with the enemy, who were led by the ablest commanders in their service; and if the Union force had the advantage of a strong position, the Confederates had that of choosing time and place, the prestige of former victories over the army of the Potomac, and of the success of the first day. Victory does not always fall to the lot of those who deserve it; but that so decisive a triumph, under circumstances like these, was gained by our troops, I would ascribe, under Providence, to the spirit of exalted patriotism that animated them, and the consciousness that they were fighting in a righteous cause.

Everett is to be credited with recognizing (if perhaps, again, romanticizing) the merciful work of the women who attended to the soldiers. He refers to them as *Sisters of Christian benevolence, ministers of compassion, Angels of pity.* They *moistened the parched tongues* and *bound the ghastly wounds* of both armies, and they carried the messages whispered from dying lips to loved ones: *Carry this miniature back to my dear wife, but do not take it from my bosom till I am gone; Tell my little sister not to grieve for me as I am willing to die for my country;* and *Oh, that my mother were here.* For these ministrations, Everett says in paragraph 38, *they have entitled themselves to our highest admiration and gratitude.* This is the orator's touch, the moral approximation deriving from Everett's sensitivity to the situation and his audience. His masterful stroke of pathos rouses and awes them even though it may stretch historical accuracy.

Turning to the arguments in the next section of the address, (paragraphs 39–47), we see that whereas Lincoln and Everett were in almost perfect agreement on the politics of their time, including the slavery issue, their Gettysburg addresses register a major difference.

Everett's arguments against the Southern secession proceed from its effect on the Union and the unique Constitutional system of government established by the ratification process. He opines that marshaling the spirits and passions of so many individuals, so many regions, so many states, into a political union such as that forged in Philadelphia was a miracle, the greatest work of any men in any age. These men were Conditores Imperiorum, he avers, Founders of States and Commonwealths. Destroying this covenant for selfish interests, he charges, is by contrast the greatest crime of any men of any age, and made worse by a supreme sophistry. The cotton states radicals are Eversores Imperiorum, Destroyers of States, and Everett assures his audience that these men shall earn the *execration of the ages* for their condemnable acts.

While Everett's arguments are grounded in preserving the Union forged by the ratification of the Constitution, Lincoln reaches further back in his address to the Declaration of Independence and its proclamations that *all men are created equal* and that their governments derive their just powers from the *consent of the governed.* Everett is talking about a political union called the *United States*; Lincoln is talking about a nation called *America.* Everett is seeking to preserve the federal government; Lincoln is seeking to preserve the idea of popular government. David Donald sees Lincoln's argument this way: liberty was not granted by the Constitution; the Constitution simply ratified an ideal that had been developing for one hundred fifty years and that was articulated in the Declaration of Independence. Lincoln, Donald claims, *drove home his belief that the United States was not just a political union, but a nation—a word he used five times* (p. 462). Bartlett also makes this critical distinction between a political union and a nation of people in his assessment of the two orations:

> *Any reasonably educated partisan of Union-first would have been impressed [by Everett's address]. Meanwhile, unhappily for Edward's reputation, but to the lasting benefit of the nation, Lincoln's brief words articulated an emerging American identity that most of his audience could not grasp*

at first hearing but which later generations would instinc-
tively understand as a classic answer to the question that
had nagged the country for years: What does it mean to be an
American? Consequently, the orator's words were forgotten,
while the president's became immortal. (p. 460)

Another way to read these two orations is to see them as equally
cogent arguments; i.e., the two Gettysburg addresses complementing
one another perfectly. The preservation of both the Union and the
nation was at stake in the Civil War. Everett's quarrels with secession
and the effect it would have on the Union were vitally important for
his day and his time, whereas Lincoln's emphasis on America as a
nation, one dedicated to the concept of equality, were important for
the future of the United States. The length of time each man took to
articulate his position is irrelevant in this context while the message
that proceeds from each speech is.

Everett continues his memorial address with a discussion of reconciliation. He consoles his audience with his knowledge that the
greatest periods of peace always seem to follow the worst periods of
war: *The violent excitement of the passions in one direction is generally*
followed by a reaction in the opposite direction. He asserts that the
North has carried on the war with full regard for Christian values, the
rule of law, and modern civilization. This humane treatment of fellow
citizens in the South will create a climate for reconciliation once the
insurrection has been put down, Everett assures his audience. He
knows, too, that most Southerners would vote for peace if given the
chance. It is in their hands that he places his faith rather than in the
hands of politicians that he himself once trusted:

> *But the hour is coming and now is, when the power of the*
> *leaders of the Rebellion to delude and inflame must cease.*
> *There is no bitterness on the part of the masses. The people*
> *of the South are not going to wage an eternal war, for the*
> *wretched pretext by which this Rebellion is sought to be justi-*
> *fied. The bonds that unite us as one people--a substantial*
> *community of origin, language, belief, and law, (the four*

great ties that hold the societies of men together;) common national and political interests; a common history; a common pride in a glorious ancestry; a common interest in this great heritage of blessings, the very geographical features of the country; the mighty rivers that cross the lines of climate and thus facilitate the interchange of natural and industrial products; .... These bonds of union are of perennial force and transient. The heart of the people, North and South, is for the Union. Indications, too plain to be mistaken, announce the fact, both in the East and the West of the States in Rebellion. In North Carolina and Arkansas the fatal charm at length is broken. At Raleigh and Little Rock the lips of honest and brave men are unsealed, and an independent press is unlimbering its artillery. When its rifled cannon shall begin to roar, the hosts of treasonable sophistry, — the mad delusions of the day --will fly like the Rebel Army though the passes of yonder mountains. The weary masses of the people are yearning to see the dear old flag again floating upon their capitals; they sigh for the return of peace, prosperity, and happiness which they enjoyed under a government whose power was felt only in its blessings.

Unnoticed by most in Everett's address is his apologia for having been blinded early in his life by the beauty and potential of what he felt the Founders had achieved and by his belief in compromise as the pathway to the slow demise of slavery. Here are those words:

A sad foreboding of what would ensue, if war should break out between North and South has haunted me through life, and led me, perhaps too long, to tread in the path of hopeless compromise, in the fond endeavor to conciliate those who were predetermined not to be conciliated.

These are hard words for Everett to utter, no doubt, but they are the words of a man of integrity. Everett is expressing that essential quality of an orator, an *honest heart,* as his mentor John Quincy Adams had put it, a quality he defined for his students as the *personal character* necessary to persuade an audience and without which *no eloquence can operate upon his belief* (1:345-48).

In his moving peroration, Everett returns to his central mission: praising the dead soldiers. In case his primary goal had been lost in his long discourse on the battles and his arguments against secession, Everett reaches deep into his education for his most eloquent passages. Perhaps Lincoln put it more succinctly when he promised that *these dead shall not have died in vain,* but Everett put it more personally and intimately:

> And now, friends, fellow-citizens of Gettysburg and Pennsylvania, and you from remoter States, let me again invoke your benediction on these honored graves. You feel, though the occasion is mournful, that it is good to be here. You feel that it was greatly auspicious for the cause of the country, that the men of the East and the men of the West, the men of nineteen sister States, stood side by side, till a clarion,—louder than that which marshaled them to the combat, shall awake their slumbers. God bless the Union;— –it is dearer to us for the blood of those brave men shed in its defense. The spots on which they stood and fell; these pleasant heights; the fertile plain beneath them; the thriving village whose streets so lately rang with the strange din of war; the fields beyond the ridge; the little streams which wind through hills, on whose banks in after-time the wondering plowman will turn up, with the rude weapons of savage warfare, the fearful missiles of modern artillery; the Seminary Ridge, the Peach-Orchard, Cemetery, Culp, and Wolf Hill, Round Top, Little Round Top, humble names, henceforward dear and famous,—no lapse of time, no distance of space, shall cause you to be forgotten. "The Whole earth," said Pericles, as he stood over the remains of his fellow citizens, who had fallen in the first year of the Peloponnesian War, "--the whole earth is the sepulcher of illustrious men." All time, he might have added, is the millennium of their glory. We bid farewell

> *to the dust of these martyr-heroes. Wheresoever through-*
> *out the civilized world the accounts of this great warfare*
> *are read, down to the latest period of recorded time, in the*
> *glorious annals of our common country there will be no*
> *brighter page than that which relates THE BATTLES OF*
> *GETTYSBURG.*

In this quotation, we see the distinctiveness of Everett's rhetoric. Where Lincoln's speech rose above particulars, Everett's descended onto the field of battle. Where Lincoln's speech is philosophical, Everett's is rhetorical. He has found, as Aristotle taught him, the available means of persuasion at a particular moment in time (Hill, p. 63). Everett's imagery takes us to this now historic place where we experience the chaos of battle, feel the pain, hear the noises, and sense the glory for which men died. Everett is the *vir bonus dicendi peritus* he was trained to be by John Quincy Adams: the good man speaking well. He is speaking words of consolation for the dead soldiers' loved ones; he is speaking words of commitment to the country; he is speaking words of conciliation to those doing battle on the other side. The result is a speech that goes to the heart of Everett's beliefs in the preservation of the community, exactly as Quintilian would have urged him to do.

Reflecting his other great memorial orations, and his appropriation of Ciceronian rhetoric, Everett's style is mixed, rising above the vernacular in those parts of the speech demanding high oratory and leveling off into the conversational when doing the work of historical accuracy. Thus, the exordium and peroration are written in a more poetic diction while the paragraphs devoted to the history of the battles as well as those containing Everett's arguments are written in a more prosaic style.

When we look critically at Everett's Gettysburg address, we understand why commentary about it is so varied. Each person viewed the event from his or her own perspective. The gentleman who complained that Everett did not spend enough time on General Reynolds's death is from General Reynolds's home town. He remembers only that. The Southern writer forgets the conciliatory remarks

and remembers only the arguments offered against the right of secession. The antiwar activist notices only the people on the platform and
the misguided policy, as he sees it, that they are pursuing, and so he
misses the essence of Everett's speech. There is enough in the speech
to rouse or ruffle every attitude. Perhaps that is its magic.

Edward Everett spoke on a few occasions after Gettysburg, but they
were anticlimactic. His oratorical career had reached its crescendo
at this historic dedication ceremony. He continued to support the
war effort to its conclusion. He supported Lincoln over McClellan
in the election of 1864, and he prayed for the day when peace would
return to his country. On January 15, 1865, suffering from what was
most likely pneumonia, Edward Everett died at his home in Boston.
Appropriate tributes were offered to him by the secretary of state,
William Seward on behalf of President Lincoln, and by the city of
Boston, the commonwealth of Massachusetts, and Harvard University.
Seward's words are perhaps the most succinct and fitting:

The President directs the undersigned to perform the painful duty
of informing the people of the United States that Edward Everett, distinguished not more by learning and eloquence than by unsurpassed
and disinterested labors of patriotism at a period of political disorder,
departed this life at four o'clock this morning. (Frothingham, p. 471)

WORKS CITED

Adams, John Quincy. Lectures on Rhetoric and Oratory. Two
vols. Reprint, Delmar, N.Y.: Scholars, 1997.

Bartlett, Irving. *Edward Everett Reconsidered,* New England
Quarterly 69, 3 (September 1996): 429–60.

Donald, David Herbert. Lincoln. New York: Simon and Schuster,
1995.

Everett, Edward. Papers. Massachusetts Historical Society.

Freidel, Frank. *Foreword,* in Edward Everett at Gettysburg.

Boston: Massachusetts Historical Society. 1963.

Frothingham, Paul Revere. Edward Everett: Orator and
Statesman. Boston: Houghton Mifflin Company. 1925.

Goodwin, Doris Kearns. Team of Rivals. New York: Simon and
Schuster Paperbacks. 2005.

Hill, Forbes. *Aristotle's Rhetorical Theory,* in A Synoptic
History of Classical Rhetoric, 3rd ed. James J. Murphy and
Richard A. Katula. Mahwah, N.J.:
Erlbaum Associates,
Inc. 2003.

Orations and Speeches on Various Occasions by Edward Everett.
Four Vols. Boston: Little, Brown, and Company. 1892.

Reid, Ronald. Edward Everett: Unionist Orator. New York:
Greenwood Press, 1990.

Tilberg, Frederick. Gettysburg National Military Park.
Washington, D.C.: Division of Publications, National Park
Service, U.S. Department of the Interior. 1962.

Varg, Paul. Edward Everett: The Intellectual in the Turmoil of
Politics. London and
Toronto: Associated University
Presses. 1992.

Wills, Garry. Lincoln at Gettysburg: The Words That Remade
America. New York: Simon and Schuster. 1992.

Epilogue

Prominent among Edward Everett's accomplishments was his role in preserving George Washington's home, Mount Vernon, by donating the proceeds of one speech, *The Character of Washington,* toward that purpose. But perhaps an even greater accomplishment was the argument he made in the speech: that George Washington was not only a great American during his lifetime but that he was the greatest man of any age. That Everett's argument was convincing is evidenced by the crowds that clamored to hear the speech, the accolades from the press, and even from his critics, and the fact that Mount Vernon was saved and remains today one of the nation's most beautiful and popular destinations.

It is now time to measure the life of Edward Everett with an emphasis on his career as an orator. The title of this book suggests an emphasis on Everett's eloquence, but the subtitle suggests even more: that he was America's greatest orator. To prove its assertion, the subtitle demands an argument, certainly not one as daunting as Everett set for himself in *Washington* but one demanding some evidence and reasoning. It is to this argument that the Epilogue now turns.

The argument for Everett's greatness can be broken into its constituent claims. First is that he was generally astute about the topics and issues that he addressed in his career. The speeches reviewed here, and the effect they had on the American public at the time, are a testament to his erudition and prescience. Vision is important in all times, but Everett's vision was particularly important to his age because it was a time of beginnings, a time when direction and focus were essential to assuring that the new nation would move forward. Devoting careful thought and thorough research to assure correctness is perhaps the defining quality of Everett's public oratory.

In addition, Edward Everett displayed throughout his oratorical career a *heart of integrity,* that very quality his mentor John Quincy Adams urged upon his students as the quintessential mark of the great orator. As we have seen, particularly at Gettysburg, Everett's oratory is never about himself; it is always about the event and the audience assembled to hear him. And he applied reason to his topics, a fact that even the most rhetorical of his flourishes never overshadowed. Everett was one of those rare individuals able to reach beyond himself to address purposes larger than his own and, in this way, to achieve the goal of all epideictic oratory: an honest accounting of his subject properly *veiled* to accommodate the circumstances in which he was speaking.

Everett was correct in choosing to become a festival orator. He might, indeed, have written a great book or a series of brilliant essays, as did many of his contemporaries, such as Emerson or Thoreau, but he understood that his talent lay in public speaking. And as we have seen, among his contemporaries he was best able to bring the intellectualism of his age to ordinary Americans in a voice of pure eloquence. And his popularity as a festival orator, as neoclassical and stately as he was in an almost old-fashioned sense, never waned. As Reid points out, Everett's collected orations were frequently reprinted even thirty years after his death (p. 56). Truthful speech, beautifully spoken, never goes out of style. Just as Washington was the right man for the right time, Edward Everett chose the right career for his.

And no other orator of any era had the intellectual breadth to speak on so many diverse topics. The nineteenth century was replete with great orators, as we have seen, but most of them spoke on one, or perhaps two, topics. Frederick Douglass, for instance, spoke on abolition and the rights of Black Americans. Daniel Webster offered some variety but spoke mostly on politics. Lucy Stone spoke on women's rights and abolition. In our own day, Martin Luther King Jr. is often cited as a great orator, and that he was. He also spoke, however, on a narrow range of topics, for the most part civil rights. John F. Kennedy, also known as a great speaker in our era, delivered three or four notable orations on diverse political topics, but even this range pales in comparison to Everett's, a man who spoke on dozens of political issues but also on religion, history, art, literature, commerce, agriculture, and science. There is no other orator of any age, save perhaps Cicero, who even approaches Everett's intellectual scope or the sheer volume of his public speeches.

Everett's orations were timely. In 1824, for instance, America was primed to develop its own identity, and Everett's Phi Beta Kappa Society oration was timed perfectly for the historical moment in which he delivered it. What followed was an era that transcended the narrow cultural compass (inspiring as it was) imposed by the teachings of the Bible; that transcended the Revolution, with the great but incomplete promises written into the Constitution; and that looked beyond the stifling traditions of European monarchy and the class consciousness that crimped and hemmed in the collective genius inherent in popular government. The tears and cheering that followed Everett's Phi Beta Kappa oration were an instinctive response to the truth. Those in attendance, and those who later read his essay, knew that Edward Everett had just revealed the future, even if it remained partially shrouded in the misty memory of the Revolution and the heroism of Lafayette.

The same may be said for all of Everett's orations: they were written for the moment in which they were to be delivered. As the heroes of the Revolution were dying, he spoke of their heroism; as the political leaders of his generation were dying, he measured their lives for the emulation of the next; during peace, he spoke of the arts, literature, science, and education; during war, he spoke of war. Appendix A reveals a true man of letters who answered the public's questions when they were asked, and in language the public could understand and appreciate.

Everett's ideas were also timeless. He was wrong in his diffidence and passivity about ending slavery but right in his understanding of it as an evil to be eradicated. It is a matter of opinion whether he was right about how to end it. America was the only nation in the modern era to go to war to end slavery. Six hundred fifty thousand Americans lost their lives in the Civil War, a war that Lincoln did not want, that most Americans did not want, but that, in the end, could not, perhaps, have been resolved peacefully. Everett's speech on the floor of Congress in 1826 remains a mystery—that words so ill chosen would have been uttered by a man so gifted with them. In this vein, he is also to be criticized for dismissing the slavery issue during his political career; it was, indeed, the cause of the war, as he admits at Gettysburg. Nevertheless, history has shown time and time again that negotiating conflicts is almost always better than fighting about them. What unspeakably painful experiences for black Americans might have been forestalled by a negotiated settlement to end slavery? What lingering resentments, some that remain even today, might have been avoided between the North and the South? There is a certain timelessness in the idea that speech is what separates us from the animals, an idea that both Cicero and Isocrates emphasized. Edward Everett clung to this belief throughout his life, even if in the crisis of slavery to a fault.

Everett was also correct about his devotion to the Constitutional Union forged in 1788. It is the most miraculous of all political deeds to draw together the infinite interests that motivate individuals and tribes of individuals under one document, fallible though it may be. To imagine a continent of two Americas, split across the middle from Maryland to California, one free and one most likely evolved into something like the apartheid world reminiscent of South Africa, is indeed frightening. The United States of America has become one of the great pillars of freedom and hope for people around the world, and its Constitution has been modeled by numerous governments seeking to form *more perfect* unions.

In a related sense, Everett was justly concerned and correct about

party and sectional faction. Whatever progress we have made as
a nation has come from those who have had the courage to look
beyond ideology to pragmatism. Parties polarize; Americans solve
problems. All of our great presidents, all of our great leaders, have
understood this basic principle. While the media today thrives on
the drama inherent in polarized discourse, right-thinking Americans
understand that it is the quiet, less hysterical discourse that gets
things done. This approach alone meets the standard of the Golden
Mean. The memory of Edward Everett reminds us that Greatness
is not found in sound-bites or in the dazzle (as he called it) of celebrity but in the power of explaining great ideas to ordinary people in
beautiful language.

Everett was right to honor the departed heroes of the past. A
learned sage writes, *Let us now praise famous men ... leaders of the
people by their counsels, ... wise and eloquent in their instructions,* for
there is nothing that so kindles the enthusiasm of young and old alike
than the memory of those who lived their lives for purposes larger
than their own. As Cicero himself declared,

> *How many images of the bravest men, carefully elaborated,
> have the Greek and Latin writers bequeathed to us, not
> merely for us to look at and gaze upon, but also for our
> imitation! And I, always keeping them before my eyes as
> examples of my own public conduct, have endeavored to
> model my mind and views by continually thinking of those
> excellent men.* [Murphy and Katula, p. 300]

In a time like ours, when so many of our leaders are villains rather
than role models and when so many of our heroes are beyond emulation, we might heed the lessons of history, as Everett did.

Edward Everett was right to speak about *faith.* Today our leaders
speak of *hope,* and that is fine, but there is a difference between *faith*
and *hope*—an important one. *Hope* is the last thread to which we
cling when all the others have frayed or broken. Faith is the assurance
that things will be as promised because there is some power or force
greater than ourselves guiding us to truth. Hope requires faith. Hope

without faith leads us to a desperate and solipsistic public rhetoric. Hope premised on faith leads to idealism. And idealism leads to optimism, that belief in the future so important to progress.

Edward Everett was right about idealism. Idealism can thrive on skepticism and criticism, but when those moods turn to cynicism, society has accepted defeat. History, as recounted in Everett's oratory, provides this lesson. The ancient Rhodians produced pottery upon which they painted chains of birds, all looking forward except for one bird, whose face turned over his shoulder. Those looking forward were the idealists; the one bird looking backward was the critic. We need both, and in the same measure.

Similarly for patriotism. Sycophantic flag waving is, of course, an idle gesture. But engaging in a lively exchange of ideas is at the heart of American democracy. Citizens trained to have the courage of their convictions while remaining open to the ideas of others are patriots. The balance and harmony in our public discourse that comes from a sense of *self interest-rightly understood,* as Tocqueville once put it, is always to be encouraged. And this Everett did.

Is there a need for great oratory today? Do we yet yearn for leaders who can inspire us to larger goals? What value is a great idea if not communicated properly? Who benefits from an idea that remains private or poorly explained? The answers to these questions are quite simple when we think about them. When we look back on the life of Edward Everett, we can see how important is education, part of which must be to train each generation in articulate speech. All the great minds throughout civilization have known this truth; we see it exemplified in the life of Edward Everett. That is his gift to us, and this is why he was, and remains, America's greatest orator.

WORKS CITED

Cicero. In Defense of the Poet Archias. In Murphy, James, and
Richard A. Katula. A Synoptic History of Classical
Rhetoric, 3rd ed. Rahwah, New Jersey: Erlbaum Publishers,
1994.

DeNormandie, James. *Oration,* Centennial Anniversary of the
Birth of Edward Everett. Dorchester Historical
Society. Boston: Rockwell and Churchill, City Printers.
1895.

Reid, Ronald. Edward Everett: Unionist Orator.
New York: Greenwood Press, 1990

Appendix A

The demonstrative speeches of Edward Everett 1815-1865

TITLE	LOCATION
April 12, 1815 *Inaugural Address,* Professor of Greek Studies	Harvard University Cambridge, Mass
Winter, 1822-1823 Repeated, 1823-1824 *Antiquities and Ancient Art*	Boston, Mass
December 19, 1823 Repeated, January 14, 1824 *Relief of the Greeks*	Boston, Mass
August 26, 1824 *The Circumstances* *Favorable to the Progress* *of Literature in America*	Cambridge, Mass

TITLE	LOCATION

December 22, 1824
*The First Settlement of
New England* — Plymouth, Mass

April 19, 1825
*The First Battles of the
Revolutionary War* — Concord, Mass

August 19, 1825
*Speech on Reinstatement
of Expelled Harvard Students* — Cambridge, Mass

July 4, 1826
*The Principles of the
American Constitution* — Cambridge, Mass

August 1, 1826
Adams and Jefferson — Charlestown, Mass

Woolens and the Tariff
June 5, 1827 — Boston, Mass
Repeated July 29, 1827 — Harrisburg, Mass

October 10, 1827
Concord Cattle Show — Concord, Mass

November 7, 1827
Repeated at least 2 times
*Importance of Scientific
Knowledge to Practical Men* — Boston, Mass

June 5, 1828
Speech for Daniel Webster — Boston, Mass

TITLE	LOCATION

July 4, 1828
The History of Liberty   Charlestown, Mass

September 18, 1828
Repeated, September 25, 1828
200*th Anniversary of the*   Salem, Mass
Landing of Governor Endicott

September 19, 1928
Lecture to Mechanics' Institute   Waltham, Mass

September 26, 1828
Monument to John Harvard   Charlestown, Mass

June 2, 1829
Speech at Nashville, Tennessee   Nashville, TN

June 17, 1829
Speech at Lexington, Kentucky   Lexington, KY

June 29, 1829
Speech at Yellow Springs   Yellow Springs, OH

August 13, 1829
The Academy   Northampton, Mass

October 7, 1829
Worcester Cattle Show   Worcester, Mass

Lecture to Mechanics' Association   Boston, Mass
Part 1, October 19, 1829,
Part 2, October 26, 1829;
Part 3, November 2, 1829

TITLE	LOCATION
October 21, 1929 *Mechanics' Association*	Boston, Mass
November 16, 1829 *Organizational Meeting of* *Middlesex County Lyceum*	Concord, Mass
November 17, 1829 *The Boyhood and Youth* *of Franklin*	Boston, Mass
January 2, 1830 *Columbia Typographical Society*	Washington DC
June 28, 1830 *The Settlement of Massachusetts*	Charlestown, Mass
July 5, 1830 *Forth of July at Lowell*	Lowell, Mass
October 6, 1830 Repeated, October 18, 1830 *The Working Men's Party*	Charlestown, Mass
October 7, 1830 *After-dinner Speech* *at Faneuil Hall*	Boston, Mass
November 2, 1830 *Lecture at Charlestown Lyceum*	Charlestown, Mass

TITLE	LOCATION
May 10, 1831 Repeated, May 11, 1831 *Present State and Prospects* *of Europe*	Salem, Mass
June 7, 1831 *Lecture*	Unknown
July 4, 1831 *After-dinner Speech*	Charlestown, Mass
October 14, 1831 *American Manufacturers*	New York, NY
October 18, 1831 *Impromptu Speech Following* *Daniel Webster*	Boston, Mass
November 14, 1831 Repeated 3 times *Advantages of Scientific* *Knowledge to Working Men*	Boston, Mass
January 16, 1832 *Colonization and Civilization* *of Africa*	Washington DC
September 14, 1832 *Meeting to select delegates* *to the state National* *Republican convention*	Charlestown, Mass
October 3, 1832 *Concord Cattle Show*	Concord, Mass

TITLE	LOCATION

October 12, 1832
Address to Massachusetts State   Worchester, Mass
National Republican convention

Lecture on Agriculture   Boston, Mass
Part 1, November 7, 1832;
Part 2, November 14, 1832

November 11, 1833
·Repeated 2 times
Election-Eve speech   Charlestown, Mass

February 5, 1833
Meeting of the American   Washington DC
Colonization Society

April 22, 1833
Meeting of the Charlestown   Charlestown, Mass
Temperance Society

April 26, 1833
Repeated 2 times
Early History of Massachusetts   Medford, Mass

May 8, 1833
Superiority of American   Unknown
Institutions to those of England

May 21, 1833
Education in the Western States   Boston, Mass

May 28, 1833
The Bunker Hill Monument   Boston, Mass

TITLE	LOCATION
June 6, 1833 *Fund Raising Speech for the* *Bunker Hill Monument*	Charlestown, Mass
June 11, 1833 *Meeting of the Middlesex County* *Temperance Society*	Concord, Mass
June 14, 1833 *Temperance*	Salem, Mass
June 17, 1833 Repeated, June 26, 1833 *Standard of Artillery*	Charlestown, Mass
June 18, 1833 *Prisons*	Unknown
June 26, 1833 Repeated 3 times *Speech for President* *Andrew Jackson*	Charlestown, Mass
July 4, 1833 *The Seven Years' War, The* *School of the Revolution*	Worcester, Mass
The Education of Mankind August 20, 1833 August 29, 1833	New Haven, CT Cambridge, Mass
October 11, 1833 *Institutions of America*	Cambridge, Mass

TITLE	LOCATION
October 16, 1833 Repeated 4 times *Agriculture*	Brighton, Mass
October 21, 1833 Repeated Unknown Number of times *Anecdotes of Early Local History*	Boston, Mass
October 24, 1833 *Lecture to the Society for the* *Diffusion of Useful Knowledge*	Boston, Mass
October 25, 1833 *Speech at an undesignated* *Temperance meeting*	Unknown
October 28, 1833 November 6, 1833 *Speech at a reception* *given for Henry Clay*	Bunker Hill, Charleston, Mass
August 7, 1834 August 13, 1834 *After-dinner speech at a* *Whig meeting*	Salem, Mass
September 6, 1834 *Eulogy on Lafeyette*	Boston, Mass
October 14, 1834 *Lecture on poisoning to* *Charleston to [MA] Lyceum*	Unknown

TITLE	LOCATION
November 7, 1834 *Speech to a Whig caucus*	Unknown
November 10, 1834 *Two short speeches...*	Boston/Charleston, Mass
Short Speech November 21, 1834 November 26, 1834	Boston, Mass Unknown
April 20, 1835 *The Battle of Lexington*	Lexington, Mass
1835 *The Youth of Washington*	Beverly, Mass
July 6, 1835 *After-dinner speech, Boston-Worcester Railroad*	Worcester, Mass
August 19, 1835 *After-dinner speech, school meeting*	Unknown
August 25, 1835 *Education Favorable to Liberty Morals, and Knowledge*	Amherst, Mass
August. 27 1835 *Lecture on Land Tenures*	Springfield, Mass
September 30, 1835 *The Battle of Bloody Brook*	South Deerfield, Mass

TITLE	LOCATION
October 7, 1835 *The Western Railroad*	Boston, Mass
Lecture on Peruvian Indians November 24, 1835 December 15, 1835	Boston, Mass Charleston Lyceum
Lecture on Mexican Indians December 1, 1835 December 29, 1835	Boston, Mass Charleston Lyceum
March 2, 1836 *After-dinner speech, the opening* *of Warren Bridge*	Boston, Mass
March 30, 1836 *After-dinner speech,* *Daniel Webster*	Boston, Mass
May 5, 1836 *Prisoners at MA* *State Prison*	Boston, Mass
May 25, 1836 *Anniversary of the Settlement* *Of Springfield*	Springfield, Mass
June 6, 1836 Repeated June 18, 1836 *The importance of the Militia*	Boston, Mass
June 17, 1836 *The Seventeenth of June at* *Charlestown, MA*	Bunker Hill

TITLE	LOCATION

July 7, 1836
After-dinner speech at a
4th of July celebration

Roxbury, Mass

July 28, 1836
A short speech

New Bedford, Mass

August 24, 1836
After-dinner speech at
Undesignated school exhibition

Unknown

September 7, 1836
Character of Lafayette

Boston, Mass

August 26, 1836
Speech to the Farm School

Thompsons Island, Mass

August 31, 1836
After-dinner speech at Harvard
College commencement

Cambridge, Mass

September 8, 1836
Harvard Centennial Anniversary

Cambridge, Mass

September 20, 1836
Speech to a militia brigade

Boston, Mass

The Settlement of Dedham
September 21, 1836
September 28, 1836
October 1, 1836

Dedham, Mass

TITLE	LOCATION
The cattle show at Danvers Sept 28, 1836 October 8, 1836	Danvers, Mass
October 11, 1836 *Review of Militia Brigade*	Northampton, Mass
October 20, 1836 *Speech at a public examination* *of an undesignated girls' school*	Unknown
October 31, 1836 *After-dinner speech*	Unknown
March 17, 1837 *The Irish Charitable Society,* *A speech commemorating the* *100th anniversary of the society*	Boston, Mass
March 20, 1837 *Speech at a meeting of the* *Mercantile Library Association*	Boston, Mass
May 30, 1837 *Improvements in Prison* *Discipline, A speech to the* *Prison Discipline Society*	Boston, Mass
June 5, 1837 *After-dinner speech* *commemorating the 199th* *anniversary of the Ancient and* *Honorable Artillery Company*	Boston, Mass

TITLE	LOCATION

June 14, 1837
After-dinner speech at a
meeting of the National Lancers Boston, Mass

August. 16, 1837
Superior and Popular Education, Williamstown, Mass
oration to the Adelphic Union
Society of Williams College

August 23, 1837
The Boston Schools, an After- Boston, Mass
dinner speech on the day of
school examinations

August 30, 1837
Speech presenting standards Boston, Mass
To the national lancers

September 20, 1837
The importance of the Mechanic Boston, Mass
arts, speech to the Mass. Charitable
mechanic Association

September 22, 1837
Review of the Militia Salem, Mass

October 30, 1837
Reception of the Sauks Boston, Mass
and Foxes, speech given at a
reception of Indian chiefs

TITLE	LOCATION
November 10, 1837 *Lecture on the history of the* *English language to society for* *the diffusion of useful knowledge*	Boston, Mass
November 21, 1837 *short speech at an* *undesignated meeting*	Worcester, Mass
November 28, 1837 *Lecture on the discovery of* *America by the Northmen to an* *unknown undesignated lyceum*	Unknown
September 28, 1838 *Lecture to Charlestown lyceum*	Charlestown, Mass
March 20, 1838 *Dr. Bowditch, a eulogy to the* *American Academy of* *Arts and Sciences*	Boston, Mass
May 30, 1838 *After-dinner speech at the* *40th anniversary of the Boston* *Light Infantry*	Boston, Mass
July 4, 1838 *Fourth of July 1838, an after* *dinner speech*	Boston, Mass
July 24, 1838 *Two speeches at a dinner* *honoring Daniel Webster*	Unknown

TITLE	LOCATION

August 16, 1838
Education, the nurture   Martha's Vineyard, Mass
of The Mind

August. 23, 1838
Festival at Exeter, delivered   Exeter, NH
in honor of the retiring principal
of Phillips Exeter Academy.

September13, 1838
Accumulation, Property, Capital,   Boston, Mass
Credit, a lecture to the Mercantile
Library Assoc.

October 10, 1838
Importance of Education   Taunton, Mass
in a Republic,

March 2, 1839
Speech at a reception for   Boston, Mass
General Scott

May 6, 1839
Speech at an undesignated dinner   Boston, Mass

June 3, 1839
Speech to the artillery   Boston, Mass
company on its election day

June 14, 1839
Speech presenting the standards   Boston, Mass
to the National Lancers

TITLE	LOCATION
July 18, 1839 *Speech at a school* *Commencement*	Cambridge, Mass
August 14, 1839 *After dinner speech at* *Faneuil Hall*	Boston, Mass
September 3, 1839 *The settlement of Barnstable* *After dinner speech at the 200th* *anniversary of the town's settlement*	Barnstable, Mass
September 5, 1839 *Normal Schools, delivered at the* *opening of the state normal* *school in Barre*	Barre, Mass
October 2, 1839 *Speech at a military review*	Boston, Mass
October 3, 1839 *Opening of the railroad* *to Springfield,*	Springfield, Mass
November 30, 1839 *The Scots' Charitable Society,* *After-dinner speech to the society*	Boston, Mass
December 31, 1839 *John Lowell, founder of the Lowell* *institute, an encomium*	Boston, Mass

TITLE	LOCATION
September 17, 1840 *Farewell speech to the Mass Lt.* *Governor and council*	Boston, Mass
March 11, 1840 *Short, impromptu speech* *to a Whig meeting*	Boston, Mass
May 14, 1840 *Speech to a Whig rally*	Boston, Mass
May 23, 1842 *Dr. Robinson's Medal, to the* *Royal Geographical Society*	London, England
May 25, 1842 *British Association at* *Manchester, to the British* *Assoc. for the Promotion of Science*	Manchester, England
July 4, 1842 *University of Cambridge,* *at a dinner after the inauguration* *of the chancellor*	Cambridge, England
July 14, 1842 *The Royal Agricultural Society* *at Bristol,*	Bristol, England
September 26, 1842 *Agricultural Society at Waltham,*	Waltham, England
October 6, 1842 *York Minster*	York, England

TITLE	LOCATION
November 9, 1842 *Lord Mayor's Day,*	London, England
Unknown *The Geological Society* *of London,*	London, England
May 6, 1843 *The Royal Academy of Art,*	London, England
unknown *Royal Literary Fund,*	London, England
July 14, 1843 *The Agricultural Society* *at Derby*	Derby, England
Sept 9 1843 *Reception at Hereford*	Hereford, England
October 13, 1843 *Saffron Waldon Agricultural* *Society, a dinner meeting*	Saffron Waldon, England
June 19, 1845 *Scientific Association* *at Cambridge*	Cambridge, England
The Pilgrim Fathers,	unknown
April 30, 1846 *University Education,* *Inaugural address as* *President of Harvard*	Cambridge, Mass

TITLE	LOCATION
August. 26, 1846 *two speeches, one at the* *commencement and one* *at the dinner, Harvard college*	Cambridge, Mass
November 6, 1846 *The New Medical College,*	Boston, Mass
The Famine in Ireland February 18, 1847 February 19, 1847 February 20, 1847	Boston, Mass
February 1, 1848 *Aid to the Colleges*	Boston, Mass
April 15, 1848 *Eulogy on John Quincy Adams*	Boston, Mass
June 27, 1848 *The Cambridge High School*	Cambridge, Mass
February 7, 1849 *Aid to the Colleges*	Boston, Mass
July 12, 1849 *Ipswich Female Academy* *at its Public Examination*	Ipswich, Mass
August 21, 1849 *American Scientific Association*	Cambridge, Mass
September 17, 1849 *The Departure of the Pilgrims*	Plymouth, Mass

TITLE	LOCATION
September 26, 1849 *Cattle Show at Dedham*	Dedham, Mass
April 19, 1850 *The Nineteenth of April* *at Concord*	Concord, Mass
May 27, 1850 Repeated May 29, 1850 *The Bible*	Boston, Mass
June 17, 1850 Repeated 3 times *Battle of Bunker Hill*	Charlestown, Mass
June 28, 1850 *Opening of the Brattle House*	Cambridge, Mass
August 3, 1850 *Cambridge High School*	Cambridge, Mass
November 4, 1850 *The Ottoman Empire*	Boston, Mass
February 22, 1851 *The Birthday of Washington*	New York, NY
August 2, 1851 *Conditions of a Good School*	Cambridge, Mass
September 19, 1851 *Beneficial Influence of Railroads*	Boston, Mass

TITLE	LOCATION

September 24, 1851
Repeated September 27, 1851
The Husbandman, Mechanic,   Lowell, Mass
and Manufacturer

Discovery of America
January 28, 1852   Boston, Mass
February 18, 1852
June 1, 1853

February 17, 1852
Treatment of Animals   Boston, Mass

April 18, 1852
Effects of Immigration   Boston, Mass

July 22, 1852
Festival of the Alumni   Cambridge, Mass
of Harvard

August 7, 1852
Education and Civilization   Cambridge, Mass

September 16, 1852
Dinner to Thomas Baring, Esq.   Boston, Mass

September 22, 1852
Dinner to Thomas Baring, Esq.   Boston, Mass
Different from above

October 7, 1852
Progress for Agriculture   Franklin, Mass
    and Norhampton, Mass

TITLE	LOCATION
October 27, 1852 Repeated 3 times *The Death of Daniel Webster*	Boston, Mass
January 18, 1853 Repeated 3 times *The Colonization of Africa*	Washington DC
July 4, 1853 Repeated 4 times *Stability and Progress*	Boston, Mass
August 1, 1853 Repeated 4 times *The Pilgrim Fathers*	Plymouth, Mass
October 6, 1853 *New Hampshire*	Manchester, NH
October 12, 1853 *Opposition to the Proposed New* *Constitution for Massachusetts*	Boston, Mass
November 23, 1853 *Reopening of a Hotel in Boston*	Boston, Mass
December 8, 1853 *Vice-President King*	Washington DC
July 4, 1855 Repeated July 6, 1855 *Dorchester in* 1630, 1776, *and* 1855	Dorchester, Mass

TITLE	LOCATION
July 23, 1855 Repeated July 24, 1855 *Boston School Festival*	Boston, Mass
July 28, 1855 *Launch of the Defender*	East Boston, Mass
Abbot Lawrence August 20, 1855 August 21, 1855 August 22, 1855	Boston, Mass
October 26, 1855 Repeated October 27, 1855 *Vegetable and Mineral Gold*	Boston, Mass
October 26, 1855 *Undesignated Agricultural Exhibition*	Boston (?), Mass
January 18, 1856 Repeated twice on January 19, 1856 *Daniel Webster as a Man*	Boston, Mass
February 22, 1856 Repeated 137 times *The Character of Washington*	Boston, Mass
April 5, 1856 *Reception in Philadelphia*	Philadelphia, PA
August 5, 1856 *Mr. Dowse's Library*	Boston, Mass

TITLE	LOCATION
August 28, 1856 Repeated 8 times *The Uses of Astronomy*	Albany, NY
October 8, 1856 Repeated twice on October 10, 1856 *George Peabody*	Danvers, Mass
November 13, 1856 *Eulogy on Mr. Dowse*	Danvers, Mass
December 4, 1856 *Eulogy of Dr. Warren to the Thursday evening club*	Boston, Mass
March 19, 1857 *Introduced to NY Legislature*	Albany, NY
April 9, 1857 *Memorial of the Franklin family, to the Mass. Historical Society*	Boston, Mass
April 22, 1857 *Academical Education*	St. Louis, MO
June 17, 1857 *The Statue of Warren*	Charlestown, Mass
October 9, 1857 *The Importance of Agriculture*	Buffalo, NY
October 12, 1857 *Speech at the Univ of Michigan*	Ann Arbor, MI

TITLE	LOCATION

November 11, 1857
Speech to the free academy　　Norwich, CT

December 22, 1857
Charitable Institutions　　Boston, Mass
and Charity

September 1, 1858
Dedication of the Public Library　　Boston, Mass

February 22, 1858
Dedication of　　Richmond, VA
Crawford's Washington

February 23, 1858
Presentation of the　　Richmond, VA
Cane of Washington

March 11, 1858
Three speeches, two to the　　Trenton, NJ
legislative houses and the third to
the students at the Normal School

April 10, 1858
short speech at the railroad station　　Charleston, SC

April 14, 1858
Speech at the orphanage　　Charleston, SC

April 15, 1858
Short speech at the RR station　　Columbia, SC

May 25, 1858
Recollections of Turkey　　Boston, Mass

TITLE	LOCATION
June 17, 1858 *Mr. Everett's oration* *on Washington*	Boston, Mass
July 5, 1858 *Washington abroad and at home*	Boston, Mass
July 5, 1858 *The Fourth of July*	Boston, Mass
August 19, 1858 *Commemorating Daniel Webster*	Boston, Mass
September 17, 1858 *Cattle show at Springfield*	Springfield, Mass
September 24, 1858 *The New York State* *Inebriate asylum*	Binghamton, NY
September 30, 1858 *Agricultural Society at Danvers*	Danvers, Mass
October 2, 1858 *Minot's Ledge Light House*	Minot's Ledge, Mass
December 7, 1858 *Eulogy on Thomas Dowse*	Cambridgeport, Mass
December 30, 1858 *Undesignated topic*	Medford, Mass
September 17, 1859 *Franklin, the Boston Boy*	Boston, Mass

TITLE	LOCATION

February. 10, 1859
Eulogy, William Hickling Prescott   Boston, Mass

February. 24, 1859
Eulogy, Henry Hallam   Boston, Mass

April 21, 1859
Speech at a reception   Jamestown, VA

May 21, 1859
Latin School Prize   Boston, Mass
Declamation, to the Boston
public Latin grammar school

June 8, 1859
Powers' Statue of Webster   Boston, Mass

June 9, 1859
Eulogy, Alexander Von Humboldt   Boston, Mass

July 22, 1859
Eulogy, Rufus Choate   Boston Mass

September 17, 1859
Daniel Webster   Boston, Mass

October 5, 1859
Welcoming speech to a military   Boston, Mass
unit from Connecticut

December 8, 1859
Union Meeting in Faneuil Hall   Boston, Mass

TITLE	LOCATION
December 15, 1859 *Eulogy, Washington Irving*	Boston, Mass
December 22, 1859 *Eliot School House*	Boston, Mass
September 12, 1860 *Eulogy, Lord Macaulay*	Boston, Mass
February 2, 1860 *Impromptu speech to a legislative committee regarding a proposed water project for Charleston, MA*	Boston, Mass
February 9, 1860 *Henry D. Gilpin, eulogy to the MA historical society*	Boston, Mass
February 21, 1860 *Speech to a legislative committee regarding a proposed water project for Charleston, MA*	Boston, Mass
April 3, 1860 *Birthday of Washington Irving*	New York, NY
May 2, 1860 *American Expedition to the Arctic Sea*	Boston, Mass
June 16, 1860 *Sanitary Convention*	Boston, Mass

TITLE	LOCATION

July 5, 1860
Vindication of
American Institutions

Boston, Mass

July 5, 1860
Encomium at a ceremonial
meeting for a Dr. Hayes

Unknown

July 19, 1860
Inauguration of President
Felton, an After-dinner speech
to a meeting of Harvard Alumni

Cambridge, Mass

September 13, 1860
Speech to the Everett Society

Boston, Mass

September 17, 1860
Everett School House dedication

Boston, Mass

Dec 11, 1860
Lecture on the history
of the steam Engine

Cambridgeport, Mass

March 1, 1861
Speech in New York

NY

March 18, 1861
Speech in Greenfield

Greenfield, Mass

April 12, 1861
Speech in Cincinnati

Cincinnati, OH

April 27, 1861
Flag-Raising in Chester Square

Boston, Mass

TITLE	LOCATION
May 8, 1861 *The Call to Arms*	Roxbury, Mass
June 13, 1861 *Daniel Dewey Barnard,* *eulogy to the MA historical society*	Boston, Mass
July 4, 1861 *The Questions of the day*	New York, NY
July 16, 1861 *Nathan Appleton, a eulogy* *to the merchants' exchange*	Boston, Mass
July 17, 1861 *Fiftieth Anniversary of* *Graduation, a speech at Everett's* *Class Reunion during the* *Harvard commencement day*	Cambridge, Mass
July 18, 1861 *The Twelfth Massachusetts* *Regiment, at the presentation* *of colors to the Webster Regiment*	Boston, Mass
July 25, 1861 *After Dinner Speech at a* *meeting of Harvard Alumni*	Cambridge, Mass
August 27, 1861 Repeated August 28, 1861 *Welcome Speech to Joseph* *Holt of Kentucky*	Boston, Mass

TITLE	LOCATION

September 12, 1861
Repeated September 13, 1861
Agriculture as Affected by War   Adams, NY

September 25, 1861
Repeated September 28, 1861
Dinner to Prince Napoleon   Boston, Mass

October 16, 1861
Repeated 59 times
The Causes and Conduct of   Boston, Mass
the Civil War

March 12, 1862
Repeated twice March 13, 1862
Cornelius Conway Felton   Harvard University
Cambridge, Mass

June 18, 1862
Speech to Students at a   Chicago, Il
High School

June 19, 1862
Speech in Chicago   Chicago, Il

July 12, 1862
Repeated July 14, 1862
The Army of the Potomac   Boston, Mass

July 16, 1862
Repeated July 17, 1862
Opportunities of   Cambridge, Mass
Harvard Students

TITLE	LOCATION

July 21, 1862
Repeated July 22, 1862
Female Education — Boston, Mass

August 5, 1862
Repeated August 7, 1862
The Duty of Crushing the Rebellion — Boston, Mass

August 27, 1862
Repeated August 28, 1862
The Demand for Reinforcements — Boston, Mass

September 9, 1862
Repeated twice September 10, 1862
The Irish Regiment — Boston, Mass

February 12, 1863
Nathan Hale — Boston, Mass

April 9, 1863
Repeated twice April 10, 1863
Inauguration of the Union Club — Boston, Mass

May 28, 1863
United States Naval Academy — Newport, RI

July 16, 1863
Repeated July 17, 1863
Harvard College in the War — Cambridge, Mass

July 20, 1863
The Education of the Poor — Boston, Mass

TITLE	LOCATION

October 15, 1863
Meeting of the Union Club   Boston, Mass

November 19, 1863
National Cemetery at Gettysburg   Gettysburg, PA

February 10, 1863
Repeated February 11, 1863
Aid to East Tennessee   Boston, Mass

March 12, 1864
The Navy in the War   Boston, Mass

March 26, 1864
Speech While Visiting a School   Boston, Mass

July 7, 1864
Russia and the United States   Boston, Mass

July 14, 1864
Josiah Quincy   Boston, Mass

July 20, 1864
The Administration of   Cambridge, Mass
President Quincy

October 19, 1864
Repeated October 20, 1864   Boston, Mass
The Duty of Supporting
the Government

November 1, 1864
Speech after a lecture by a visiting   Boston, Mass
Professor from Oxford

TITLE	LOCATION

November 8, 1864
Repeated November 9, 1864
Election Day Speech   Boston, Mass

November 9, 1864
Repeated November 10, 1864
The Sailors' Home   Boston, Mass

November 10, 1864
Reception of Captain Winslow   Boston, Mass

November 16, 1864
President Lincoln   Boston, Mass

December 7, 1864
Massachusetts Electoral   Boston, Mass
College of 1864

December 17, 1864
Meeting of the Union Club   Boston, Mass

Twice on January 9, 1865
The Relief of Savannah   Boston, Mass

Index

Credits

About the author

Richard A. Katula is Professor of Communication Studies at Northeastern University. Professor Katula received his Ph.D. in rhetorical studies at the University of Illinois, 1974. He has written three other books, most recently A Synoptic History of Classical Rhetoric (Erlbaum, 2003). He has also written and produced an award-winning documentary, The Gettysburg Address: A Speech for the Ages (2000). Professor Katula is a two-time Fulbright Scholar to Greece, and Director of a National Endowment for the Humanities Landmarks in American History workshop entitled, *The American Lyceum: The Rhetoric of Idealism, Opportunity, and Abolition.* Professor Katula received a 2008 Distinguished Faculty Grant from Northeastern University for this book on Edward Everett.

Other works by Richard A. Katula

A Synoptic History of Classical Rhetoric

with James J. Murphy

ISBN: 1-880393-34-4
ISBN: 1-880393-35-2 (pbk.)

The Gettysburg Address: A Speech for the Ages

A Video Documentary

RKatula@cox.net